RHUBARB RENAISSANCE

Minnesota Historical
Society Press

RHUBARB RENAISSANCE

KIM ODE

the *N*orthern plate

www.mhspress.org

The Minnesota Historical Society Press is a member of the Association of American University Presses.

Manufactured in the United States of America

10 9 8 7 6 5 4 3 2 1

♾ The paper used in this publication meets the minimum requirements of the American National Standard for Information Sciences— Permanence for Printed Library Materials, ANSI Z39.48-1984.

International Standard Book Number
ISBN: 978-0-87351-851-2 (paper)

LIBRARY OF CONGRESS CATALOGING-IN-PUBLICATION DATA
Ode, Kim, 1955–
Rhubarb renaissance / Kim Ode.
    p. cm.—(The northern plate)
Includes index.
ISBN 978-0-87351-851-2 (pbk. : alk. paper)
1. Cooking (Rhubarb) 2. Cookbooks. I. Title.

TX803.R58O34 2012
641.6'548—dc23

2011041368

....

Rhubarb Renaissance was designed and set in type by Cathy Spengler. The typefaces are Chaparral, TheSans and Basuto.

For John, who never once rolled his eyes at the dinner table

....

CONTENTS

RHUBARB—NAUGHTY and NICE ◊ 3

APPETIZERS, SALADS, and SIDE DISHES ◊ 13

ENTRÉES ◊ 31

DESSERTS ◊ 55

BREADS ◊ 101

BEVERAGES ◊ 109

INDEX ◊ 114

RHUBARB RENAISSANCE

RHUBARB—
NAUGHTY
and NICE

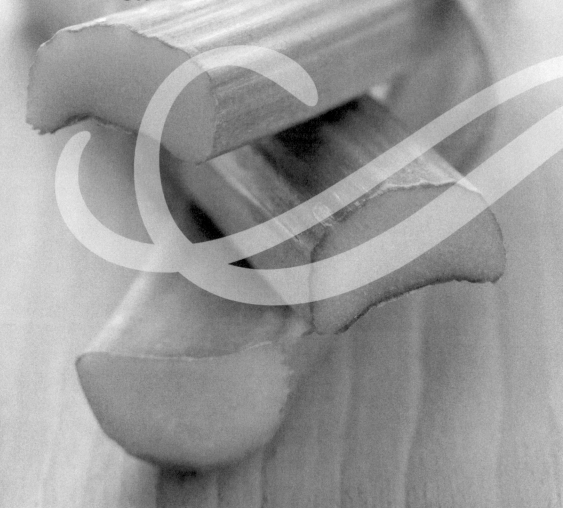

should have known better. My cousin's seemingly casual invitation was too intent on success, the gleam in her eye a bit too bright. "Take a bite," she said, holding out the stalk of rhubarb.

She spoke as if she were postponing her own pleasure, as if her bite of the scarlet stalk could wait if it meant her own dear young cousin could be happy. The rhubarb looked tasty. The pale green stalk looked like celery, but better, with brilliant red striations that caught the sunlight. The bottom knob of the stalk, where it had been pulled from the plant with a firm tug, appeared as polished as marble. This knob was pink, as pink as the hollyhocks against my Grandma Torkelson's house. It was a shade of pink that, yet today, makes me smile. But it was the other end, where the great leaf had been lopped off by my beguiling cousin, that revealed the stalk's pale green interior. "Take a bite," she said again.

I suspect that we were not unobserved—that the grownups were looking out from the kitchen at the ancient drama being enacted. For surely, generation upon generation has tempted its younger members with the suggestion that biting into a stalk of rhubarb is a delight. I mean, my cousin wasn't that original. Nor was I when, in later summers, I would extend a stalk of rhubarb toward some unsuspecting cousin, friend, neighbor kid—whoever had not experienced the stop-action surprise of a bite.

To a child's fairly untested taste buds, rhubarb is a shock. The initial crunch is quickly replaced by the sensation of every pore in your mouth constricting in the face not so much of a taste that is sour—although your brain is screaming "Sour!"—as in the realization that spitting out the rhubarb risks releasing even more of its barbarity and that, while ridding yourself of this morsel now is more important than anything you've ever done, the specter of tasting more rhubarb, even on its way out, is akin to realizing that someone's nails are only halfway down the blackboard.

In short, this drama is great good fun for the proferrers of rhubarb and an unforgettable experience for those who, against all of their instincts, finally take a bite.

The good news is that we know now that kids' taste buds are especially sensitive to bitter or sour flavors and that maturity brings the joy of realizing that rhubarb is one of the great delights of horticulture. Sadly, some people never move beyond that childhood trauma. They believe rhubarb is practically inedible unless buried in vast quantities of sugar. That's one reason rhubarb most often ends up in desserts. And, while rhubarb pie is the stuff of legend—one bite can make you realize "maybe things aren't as bad as you thought," as counseled by *A Prairie Home Companion*—the sugary treatment is just one hemisphere of the world of rhubarb.

Many of the recipes in this cookbook also explore the far side of the culinary world—a landscape where rhubarb regains its stature as a vegetable, providing a piquant accompaniment to grilled meats and succulent fish and seafood and perfectly complementing the richness of cheese. Rhubarb pickles are a revelation in salads. A cheese strudel brightens with a smear of savory rhubarb mostarda. And wait until you taste what happens when you pair rhubarb with shrimp.

In fact, I'm here to tell you right now that the more than fifty recipes in this book constitute a mostly strawberry-free zone. Well, almost. I'm not crazy. But even the classic strawberry-rhubarb pie's flavors meld more deeply with a shot of balsamic vinegar. In short, it's time for rhubarb to shed its image as a sugar-swathed pie plant and find a place at our tables as an appetizer, cocktail, salad, side dish, and entrée—while also remaining one of the best desserts around.

You'll still need to pucker up, though. After serving some of these dishes, you're going to be fielding some kisses.

WHAT IS RHUBARB?

With a nod toward rhubarb skeptics, the stalk's first primary use was not as food but as medicine. The plant's roots are in China and Tibet, with records dating back to 2700 BC showing that rhubarb's laxative qualities were used to treat constipation. Not until centuries later is there a record of it being cultivated for food in Europe. Its eventual appearance in European countries was due to its medicinal properties, but cooks apparently also were intrigued enough by its tart flavor that they began growing it around 1600. Trade routes continued to shrink the globe, and by the late 1700s imported sugar became plentiful and affordable, which pretty much lit the fuse on rhubarb's becoming more commonly referred to as "pie plant."

Botanically, rhubarb belongs to the genus *Rheum* and the plant family *polygonaceae*, the Greek "goni," meaning knee or joint, referring to the pink knob at the stem end of rhubarb stalks. And, despite being legally classified as a fruit in the United States in 1947, it is a vegetable. Its leaves contain high concentrations of oxalic acid and are toxic if eaten.

COOKING AND BAKING WITH RHUBARB

Rhubarb is a vegetable most often used as a fruit. Part of that practice springs from rhubarb's tart nature, which we seek to temper with sweeteners, whether sugar, honey, maple syrup, or other fruits. The results are legend: a rhubarb pie that signals the turn from spring into summer, or a cobbler paired with ruby-red strawberries. But rhubarb's tartness also can be exploited by giving it a sort of makeover

with more savory treatments—plying it with herbs, pairing it with meats, melding it with onions or bacon or seafood. Even savory treatments are enhanced with a bit of sugar, though; the trick is paring down the proportions to hit the right note.

Rhubarb is almost 95 percent water, which affects how it's prepared. In researching recipes for this book, I found that many called for too much cooking liquid, perhaps because the initial heating of a pot of rhubarb with only a little additional water, juice, or wine results in more sizzle than a cook may think right. But rhubarb also breaks down quite quickly. Given medium heat and a few watchful stirs, you can get past the sizzle part in no time, and the eventual result is far less soupy and far more rhubarby.

Just as we've grown accustomed to roasting vegetables to intensify their flavor, so rhubarb is enhanced by a short trip through a hot oven. Two Foundation Recipes for sweet and savory roasted rhubarb provide the basis for several recipes here but also stand alone as a quick way to prepare rhubarb for use as a sauce for ice cream or as a condiment for a backyard barbecue. Once roasted—and this takes only about twenty minutes—the rhubarb can be frozen for up to six months. Just make sure it's labeled as to whether it received the savory or sweet treatment.

Sweet Roasted Rhubarb is just that: stalks of rhubarb sprinkled with confectioners' sugar and roasted until soft, the sugar melting into the stalks.

Savory Roasted Rhubarb calls for a little sweetening, most often with maple syrup, then is roasted along with herbs (thyme and rosemary are nice) and a pinch of cayenne pepper and salt. As you can see from the description, the flavors of savory rhubarb are open to preference. If you don't have maple syrup (and it must be the real stuff), then use brown sugar. Not fond of rosemary? Try some sage or marjoram. Want to up the ante on heat? Halve and de-seed a small jalapeño, then roast and puree that with the rhubarb.

With these two basic preparations in hand, rhubarb lends its distinctive flavor to a wide range of dishes.

FREEZING RHUBARB

While rhubarb is most associated with the first flavors of spring, many varieties can be harvested into the fall. Rhubarb also is a breeze to freeze. In fact, it's possible to simply wash it, cut it into inch-long pieces, and pile it into freezer bags, leaving about a half inch of headspace before sealing tightly. Handled this way, it's best used within four months.

To better preserve the rhubarb's color and flavor, blanch the washed and cut rhubarb by plunging it into boiling water for one minute, then into ice water for another minute. An easy way to do this is by lowering a strainer or colander of rhubarb into both the boiling and icy waters. Let the rhubarb drain, then arrange it in a single layer on a tray and place in the freezer until it's frozen solid, about two hours. Then transfer it to freezer bags and freeze for six to eight months, which should get you through the winter.

FOUNDATION RECIPE FOR SWEET ROASTED RHUBARB

   3 cups rhubarb, cut in 1-inch pieces

  ⅓ cup confectioners' sugar

Preheat oven to 375 degrees. Place rhubarb in a shallow baking dish, such as a pie plate, and sprinkle confectioners' sugar evenly over fruit. Roast for 20 minutes, stirring once, until rhubarb is very soft. (Late summer rhubarb may have less moisture than the first rhubarb of spring, so watch carefully, adding a tablespoon of water if it seems to be scorching before it's soft.)

Serve as is on ice cream, or scrape into a bowl and stir briskly to break down the rhubarb into a smooth puree for use in the recipes that follow. **MAKES ABOUT 1 CUP PUREE.** ◇

FOUNDATION RECIPE FOR SAVORY ROASTED RHUBARB

    3   cups rhubarb, cut in 1-inch pieces
    ¼   cup real maple syrup
    ½   teaspoon dried thyme
    ¼   teaspoon dried rosemary
        pinch cayenne pepper
        pinch salt

Preheat oven to 375 degrees. Place rhubarb in a shallow baking dish, such as a pie plate, and drizzle with syrup. Sprinkle with thyme, rosemary, cayenne, and salt. Roast for 20 minutes, stirring once, until rhubarb is very soft. (Late summer rhubarb may have less moisture than the first rhubarb of spring, so watch carefully, adding a tablespoon of water if it seems to be scorching before it's soft.)

Serve as is alongside grilled meats, or scrape into a bowl and stir briskly to break down the rhubarb into a smooth puree for use in the recipes that follow. **MAKES ABOUT 1 CUP PUREE.** ◇

APPETIZERS, SALADS, and SIDE DISHES

ne of rhubarb's best attributes in savory dishes is in providing a tart nuance to the main flavors. Pickled rhubarb comes together in minutes and can be served alongside other pickled vegetables or as a fresh burst of flavor in salads. As part of a compote, it perfectly complements sweet shrimp or creamy cheeses. Its bright flavor revs up many side dishes and, depending on the variety, lends a sparkle of color to a plate.

SHRIMP IN KIMONOS

You've heard of pigs in blankets? Well, here's the seafood version, succulent shrimp paired with a savory rhubarb compote, then enrobed in wonton wrappers and fried. Leaving the tails on makes for prettier presentation, but tails off means easier eating. **MAKES 30–36.**

- 1 tablespoon red wine vinegar
- ⅓ cup packed light brown sugar
- 1 cup rhubarb, cut in half-inch pieces
- 1 teaspoon freshly grated ginger
- 2 scallions, white and some green parts, thinly sliced
- ¼ teaspoon dried rosemary
- 1 bay leaf
- 1½ pounds large (20–24 count) shrimp, shelled and deveined
- 1 teaspoon cornstarch
- 30–36 wonton wrappers
- 1 egg, beaten
- 1½ cups canola or peanut oil for frying
- sea salt

In a medium saucepan, combine vinegar, brown sugar, rhubarb, ginger, scallions, rosemary, and bay leaf and bring to a boil. Reduce heat to a simmer and cook, stirring occasionally, until the rhubarb breaks down and begins to look "jammy," 10 to 15 minutes. Remove from heat, remove and discard bay leaf, and scrape mixture into a bowl. Set aside to cool.

Pat shrimp dry. Sprinkle a plate with cornstarch to keep the "kimonos" from sticking after they're wrapped.

Brush one wonton wrapper with beaten egg. Place a half teaspoon of rhubarb in the center and place one shrimp on the diagonal. Fold one half of the wrapper over the shrimp, then the other. Bring the corner opposite the tail up and over the seam and pinch to seal. Pinch the remaining corner around the shrimp's tail, almost like a collar. Place on the cornstarch-covered plate and repeat until all the shrimp are wrapped.

Heat oil in a skillet or wok over medium-high heat until a wrapper starts to sizzle when you dip a corner into the oil. Fry 3 wrapped shrimp at a time for about a minute, turning once, until crisp and golden. Remove to paper towels and sprinkle with a bit of sea salt. Repeat with remaining shrimp. They're best served immediately but will hold for up to 30 minutes, uncovered, in a 200-degree oven. ◊

Rhuba-dillas

The beauty of quesadillas is that they're quick to prepare and easy to adjust to individual tastes. The balance of tart, sweet, hot, and cheesy flavors can be varied with each tortilla. MAKES 4 (8-INCH) QUESADILLAS.

8 (8-inch) flour tortillas

cooking spray

2–3 cups shredded cheese, farmer or mozzarella

¾ cup finely chopped rhubarb

½ cup finely chopped pineapple, preferably fresh

2–3 jalapeño peppers, seeded and minced

This isn't a recipe so much as a formula. Ballpark figures? For each quesadilla, plan on 2 tablespoons or so each of rhubarb and pineapple, with jalapeños to taste, along with a half cup of shredded cheese.

Lightly coat one side of a tortilla with cooking spray and place oiled-side down on a hot griddle. Top with a quarter cup of cheese, the rhubarb, pineapple, and peppers, and then another quarter cup of cheese. Cover with second tortilla.

Cook until the bottom of the tortilla begins to turn golden and the cheese is melting. Lightly spray the top of the quesadilla and carefully flip over to brown the other side. When golden, remove to cutting board and slice into wedges. Repeat process with remaining ingredients. ◊

CROSTINI WITH GOAT CHEESE, PROSCIUTTO, AND RHUBARB CHUTNEY

This appetizer is great for easy entertaining because all the components can be prepared ahead of time and then the crostini can be assembled at the last minute. I like to use La Quercia prosciutto, which is made in Iowa and has gained an international reputation. **MAKES ABOUT 3 DOZEN CROSTINI.**

½ cup packed light brown sugar

1 tablespoon rice vinegar

1 clove garlic, minced

1 teaspoon minced fresh ginger

2 teaspoons minced jalapeño pepper

1½ cups rhubarb, cut in 1-inch pieces

¼ cup finely chopped dried apricots

⅓ cup goat cheese

⅓ cup light cream cheese

1 or 2 baguettes, to make about 36 (half-inch-thick) slices

6 ounces prosciutto, cut in 1-inch widths

Stir sugar and vinegar in a small heavy saucepan over medium heat until sugar dissolves. Add garlic, ginger, and pepper and cook for 1 minute. Stir in rhubarb and apricots and continue cooking, stirring frequently, until rhubarb begins to break down and mixture begins to look "jammy," about 10 to 15 minutes. Cool to room temperature.

Preheat oven to 450 degrees. Stir together goat cheese and cream cheese. Toast baguette slices until golden, about 5 to 7 minutes, turning once. Spread with cheese and top with a dollop of rhubarb and a curl of prosciutto. Serve at once. ◊

BAKED CAMEMBERT WITH RHUBARB COMPOTE

This spicy-tart compote complements the cheese's richness. Using frozen rhubarb, this makes a lovely appetizer for winter parties, especially if you swap pistachios for the walnuts. And—trivia alert—Salvador Dali once said that the melting watches of The Persistence of Memory *were inspired by oozing Camembert. Brie works, too, but then it's good-bye, Dali.*
SERVES 6–8.

1 (4–6 inch) whole Camembert

1 teaspoon brandy or ruby port

Foundation Recipe for Savory Roasted Rhubarb (page 12),
    prepared with an additional 1 cup chopped Granny Smith
    apple and 1 tablespoon brandy or ruby port

½ cup candied walnuts, roughly chopped (recipe follows)

crusty bread

Preheat oven to 350 degrees. Unwrap the cheese and carefully slice off the thin top layer of rind. Pierce several times with a fork and sprinkle with 1 teaspoon brandy or port. Place cheese in a shallow, heatproof dish; then spoon rhubarb mixture over and around the cheese. Bake for 5 to 7 minutes, until cheese begins to soften. Sprinkle with candied walnuts. Serve immediately with crusty bread.

Candied Walnuts: Place a sheet of parchment paper on a baking sheet and set aside. Combine ½ cup water and ½ cup packed brown sugar in a saucepan and bring to a boil, stirring until sugar dissolves. Add 1 cup walnut halves and continue to stir for about 5 minutes, until mixture begins to thicken. Pour out onto parchment paper, separating the walnuts with a fork or chopstick. Sprinkle with ¼ teaspoon salt. Cool completely. Store in an airtight container at room temperature for up to a month. ◇

IN THE PINK SHRIMP SALAD

This dish reminds me of a retro "ladies lunch" salad, nestled in a leaf of butter or romaine lettuce. Pomegranate molasses is in many ethnic food aisles now and lends an inimitable depth of flavor. If you have none, proceed without it. This recipe should be started at least four hours before you intend to eat. **SERVES 4.**

PICKLED RHUBARB:

- 1 cup rhubarb, cut in quarter-inch pieces
- ¼ cup sherry vinegar
- ¼ cup rice wine vinegar
- ½ cup honey
- 1 teaspoon pomegranate molasses
- 1 teaspoon salt

Place rhubarb in a shallow heatproof bowl. In a small saucepan, combine remaining ingredients and bring to a boil. Pour over rhubarb and let sit at room temperature for at least 3 hours before using. The pickles are even better if refrigerated overnight. Any leftover pickling liquid can be refrigerated for future use.

>>

DRESSING:

½ cup low-fat mayonnaise

¼ cup low-fat sour cream

2–3 tablespoons pickling liquid from rhubarb, to taste

salt and pepper, to taste

....

Combine all ingredients and place in refrigerator for at least 1 hour to marry flavors.

SALAD:

1½ pounds large (20–24 count) shrimp, shelled and deveined

1½ cups thinly sliced celery

¼ cup finely chopped red onion

¼ cup chopped flat-leaf parsley

½ cup slivered almonds

butter or romaine lettuce

....

Bring a large pan of water to a boil. Cook shrimp until bright pink, about 3 to 5 minutes. Drain and rinse with cold water.

Toss together shrimp, celery, onion, and parsley. Dress with salad dressing, beginning with half the dressing and then adding as much as suits you. Gently fold in drained pickled rhubarb. Cover well and refrigerate for at least 1 hour.

In a small saucepan over medium heat, toast slivered almonds, watching carefully and stirring occasionally until they begin to color, about 5 minutes. Set aside. When ready to serve the salad, taste and correct seasoning, if necessary. Spoon salad into lettuce leaves, and top with toasted almonds. ◊

Confetti Salad of Kale and Rhubarb

I love this salad. It's gorgeous, but it also makes you feel like a superhero with all of its vitamins! Lacinato kale—a dark green variety often called dinosaur kale—provides the best color contrast for the ruby bits of rhubarb and golden batons of cheese. The liquid from the pickled rhubarb helps make the vinaigrette. Prepare the rhubarb at least three hours before serving. **SERVES 6.**

PICKLED RHUBARB:

1 cup rhubarb, cut in quarter-inch pieces

⅓ cup sugar

½ cup white balsamic vinegar

½ teaspoon salt

½ teaspoon mustard seeds

Place rhubarb in a shallow heatproof bowl. In a small saucepan, combine remaining ingredients and bring to a boil; cook until sugar dissolves. Pour mixture over the rhubarb and let sit at room temperature for at least 3 hours before using. The pickles' flavor even improves if refrigerated overnight. Any leftover pickling liquid can be refrigerated for future use.

SALAD:

1 bunch (12–15 leaves) Lacinato kale

3 tablespoons pickling liquid from rhubarb

3 tablespoons walnut oil

hefty pinch salt

several grinds pepper

4 ounces aged Gouda, cut in fat matchsticks (about 1 cup)

1 tablespoon butter

½ cup fresh bread crumbs, preferably sourdough

½ cup candied walnuts (page 18), roughly chopped

....

Remove center rib from kale leaves, stack several pieces, then slice crosswise into a fine julienne. You should end up with about 5 cups. Rinse kale and pat dry between paper towels or use a salad spinner.

Whisk together pickling liquid and walnut oil. Season with salt and pepper. Toss dressing with the kale, then gently fold in the cheese and drained rhubarb. Place in refrigerator for at least 30 minutes so the kale softens a bit; it can chill for up to 3 hours.

Heat butter in a small saucepan over medium heat, then add bread crumbs, stirring to coat. Cook, stirring, until crumbs are golden and crisp. Set aside.

Before serving, toss salad again, add bread crumbs and walnuts, and toss once more. ◇

Spiced Couscous with Rhubarb and Figs

This easy side dish makes the most of the contrast between sweetly exotic figs and tart homely rhubarb. It's great with grilled chicken, and any leftovers can be tossed together for lunch the next day. Be sure to remove the tough bit of stem at the tip of each dried fig before chopping. **SERVES 4.**

....

1	tablespoon canola oil
1	medium onion, chopped (about 1 cup)
½	cup chopped dried mission figs
½	cup finely chopped rhubarb
1	cup couscous
1¼	cups chicken stock
½	teaspoon salt
¼	teaspoon cinnamon
	pinch ground cloves
⅓	cup slivered almonds

....

Heat oil in medium saucepan with a tight-fitting lid. Add onions and cook, stirring, until they begin to color and soften, about 10 minutes. Add figs and rhubarb and cook 2 minutes more. Add couscous, stock, salt, cinnamon, and cloves. Bring to a boil, then cover and remove from heat. Let sit for 10 minutes, until all the liquid is absorbed. Stir in almonds and serve immediately. ◇

Rhubarb Corn Fritters

These sweet-tart nuggets make a great side dish when the first ears of sweet corn come in. Frozen corn works fine, too, but look for the small "shoepeg" variety. **MAKES ABOUT 2 DOZEN (2-INCH) FRITTERS.**

3–4 ears fresh sweet corn, to yield 2 cups kernels (see headnote)

½ cup finely chopped rhubarb

¼ cup milk

2 large eggs, beaten

3 tablespoons snipped fresh chives

1 teaspoon sugar

1 teaspoon snipped fresh dill

1 teaspoon salt

several grinds pepper

¼ cup cornmeal

½ cup flour

½ teaspoon baking powder

3 tablespoons canola oil

sour cream or maple syrup, optional

Preheat oven to 200 degrees. Slice corn from cobs and place in a medium bowl. With the dull side of a knife, scrape the cobs over the bowl to capture all the corn "milk." Add rhubarb, milk, eggs, chives, sugar, dill, salt, and pepper. Stir to mix well.

>>

In a small bowl, whisk together cornmeal, flour, and baking powder. Stir into vegetable mixture, adding a tablespoon of milk if the mixture is too dry or a tablespoon of flour if too soupy, depending on how "milky" the corn was.

In a large skillet, heat oil over medium heat. Drop batter by rounded tablespoons into the oil and fry until golden, about a minute on each side. Transfer to paper towel–lined baking sheet and keep warm in a 200-degree oven while making the rest of the fritters, adding more oil if necessary. Serve fritters with a dollop of sour cream swirled with some fresh dill, or drizzle with maple syrup. ◊

Yorkshire Rhubarb

My friend Cindy Jurgenson lent me one of her old cookbooks from "the good cooks of Litchville, North Dakota," which was full of rhubarb recipes. Most were familiar, but one was a variation on the savory Yorkshire puddings served with roast beef. That cook had made it into a dessert, but this variation returns it to side dish territory. **SERVES 6–8.**

2 eggs

¾ cup milk

¾ cup flour

½ teaspoon salt

½ teaspoon dried thyme, or 1 teaspoon fresh

2 slices bacon, cut in half-inch pieces

1½ cups rhubarb, cut in half-inch pieces

¼ cup packed light brown sugar

In a blender, combine eggs, milk, flour, salt, and thyme. Process until smooth. Set aside for 30 minutes.

Preheat oven to 425 degrees. Slowly fry bacon in a 10-inch ovensafe pan (cast iron is ideal, but see note, below). Remove bacon from pan and drain on paper towels. Reheat the rendered bacon fat until sizzling, then pour the batter into the pan. Scatter rhubarb over the batter, then sprinkle with brown sugar and bacon.

Bake for 25 to 30 minutes, until crust is nicely browned. Cut in wedges and serve alongside any roasted meat or poultry.

Note: If you don't have an ovensafe pan, pour the bacon renderings into a similarly sized baking dish, then proceed with the recipe as directed. ◇

Rhubarb-Bacon Compote

Sure, you can't go wrong with bacon and onions, but rhubarb ups the ante in this piquant compote. It's great alongside pork tenderloin but would also jazz up grilled bratwurst or chicken breasts. **MAKES ABOUT 1 CUP.**

- 2 slices thick-cut bacon
- 1 cup finely minced yellow onion
- 1 cup thinly sliced rhubarb
- 3 tablespoons maple syrup
- 1½ tablespoons red wine vinegar
- pinch allspice
- pinch dried thyme

In a skillet over medium heat, brown the bacon until crisp, then set aside on paper towels. Add the onion to the bacon drippings and cook, stirring, until soft and lightly golden, about 7 to 10 minutes. Stir in rhubarb, then add the maple syrup, vinegar, allspice, and thyme and cook over low heat until rhubarb is soft, about 5 minutes. Remove from heat and crumble bacon into the rhubarb. Serve with grilled meats or poultry. ◊

Rhubarb Ketchup

This condiment is terrific on sandwiches, especially turkey or ham, but also is great served on grilled burgers or other meats. As with traditional ketchup, it provides a great dunking sauce; my family likes this with crispy roasted potato wedges. This ketchup may be refrigerated for up to two weeks and also may be frozen for up to six months. **MAKES ABOUT 2 CUPS.**

- 4 cups rhubarb, cut in 1-inch pieces
- 3 cups diced yellow onion
- 1 cup packed dark brown sugar
- 1 cup granulated sugar
- 1 cup apple cider vinegar
- 1 (28-ounce) can diced tomatoes, preferably a fire-roasted organic variety
- 2 teaspoons salt
- 1 teaspoon dry mustard
- ½ teaspoon celery seed
- ½ teaspoon ground cloves
- ¼ teaspoon red pepper flakes
- 1 cinnamon stick

In a heavy pot, combine all ingredients and bring to a boil over medium heat, stirring frequently. Reduce heat and simmer for about 1 hour, until the rhubarb breaks down. Check frequently to make sure nothing scorches.

Remove cinnamon stick, and let mixture cool for about an hour. Spoon two-thirds of the mixture into a blender and puree until smooth, then stir back into cooked mixture. For less texture, puree the entire mixture. ◇

BROWNED BUTTER RHUBARB SAUCE

Butter is wonderful, of course, but melting it to the point where it begins to turn brown adds a nutty nuance to sauces. This one is wondrous on vegetables of every season, whether roasted or steamed. Plus, its pale pink blush looks especially gorgeous when drizzled over beets, cauliflower, or broccoli. **MAKES ABOUT 1½ CUPS.**

⅓ cup pomegranate juice

1 cup finely chopped rhubarb

1 tablespoon Dijon mustard

1 shallot, sliced

¼ cup honey

¼ teaspoon salt

few grinds fresh pepper

8 tablespoons (1 stick) unsalted butter

In a blender, combine juice, rhubarb, mustard, shallot, and honey. Puree until smooth, stopping to scrape down the sides. Add salt and pepper and blend.

In a small heavy saucepan over low heat, melt the butter and cook until the solids separate and it begins to turn brown. Watch this carefully; you don't want the butter to burn. Aim for the light brown color of hazelnuts. Pour butter into a heatproof measuring cup.

With the blender running on medium speed, slowly add the butter until it's completely incorporated into the rhubarb puree. Check seasonings and adjust if necessary. Use immediately, or hold at room temperature for several hours. If refrigerated, warm over very low heat before using. ◇

ENTRÉES

nce you get your head around rhubarb being a vegetable, it's easier to think of it finding a place alongside a meal's main dish. That said, think of it as a perfect accessory— the string of pearls to a little black dress, a vivid scarf to a fisherman's knit sweater, a cool app to an iPhone. In a salsa, rhubarb plays well with tropical fruits. In a spicy mostarda, it elevates a cheese strudel. Rhubarb pairs especially well with pork and chicken and unexpectedly well with fish.

HALIBUT SKEWERS WITH MANGO-RHUBARB SALSA

You can also substitute swordfish or tuna in this recipe. The vivid colors of the salsa brighten any plate. I serve this with coleslaw and sweet corn in the summer. **SERVES 4.**

8	skewers
¾	cup fresh orange juice
⅓	cup fresh lime juice
¼	cup dry white wine
¾	cup olive oil, divided
2	large cloves garlic, crushed
1	tablespoon cumin
½	teaspoon salt
	several grinds pepper
1½	pounds halibut steaks or fillets, cut in 2-inch pieces

1 firm ripe mango, peeled and cut in quar-inch cubes

¾ cup fresh rhubarb, cut in quarter-inch cubes

¾ cup chopped cilantro leaves

2 tablespoons finely chopped red pepper

2 tablespoons finely chopped red onion

1 medium jalapeño pepper, seeded and minced

1 teaspoon honey

½ lime

....

If using wooden skewers, soak in water for at least 30 minutes.

In a sealable plastic bag, combine juices, wine, ½ cup olive oil, garlic, cumin, salt, and pepper. Add halibut to bag. Seal and turn several times to coat. Marinate, refrigerated, for at least 15 but no more than 30 minutes.

In the meantime, toss together mango, rhubarb, cilantro, red pepper, onion, jalapeño, honey, and remaining ¼ cup olive oil. Set aside so flavors can meld.

Preheat grill or broiler to medium-high heat. Remove fish from marinade; discard marinade. Thread halibut onto skewers. Place on grill or broiler pan and cook, 5 to 6 inches from the heat, for 4 to 5 minutes or until halibut is opaque throughout and flakes easily. Place on serving platter and squeeze lime juice over all. Serve 2 skewers per person, with salsa alongside. ◇

SMOKED MOZZARELLA STRUDEL WITH RHUBARB MOSTARDA

I first tasted the condiment called mostarda *at an Italian deli in the Twin Cities and loved the sweet-hot combo of fruits and mustard. Rhubarb is a natural variation, making a mostarda that's the perfect complement to a ricotta-based strudel. This combination makes a great light lunch paired with a green salad.* **SERVES 4.**

....

MOSTARDA:
This condiment also is wonderful as part of a cheese plate or with any grilled meat. The recipe makes enough for 2 strudels.

- 2 cups rhubarb, cut in half-inch pieces
- ¼ cup finely minced red onion
- ¼ cup chopped dried mission figs
- ½ cup dry white wine
- ⅓ cup sugar
- 1 tablespoon white balsamic vinegar
- 1 tablespoon mustard seeds
- 2 teaspoons dry mustard

....

Place the rhubarb, onion, figs, wine, sugar, and vinegar in a saucepan and simmer gently for about 15 minutes, stirring frequently. Add mustard seeds and dry mustard and continue to simmer until the mixture is thick and syrupy, another 10 minutes. Set aside to cool.

STRUDEL:

　1　large egg, beaten

　1　cup grated smoked mozzarella cheese

　½　cup whole milk ricotta cheese

　½　teaspoon salt

　8　sheets phyllo pastry, thawed

　3　tablespoons butter, melted

　¼　cup freshly grated Parmesan cheese

....

Preheat oven to 425 degrees. In a medium bowl, stir together egg, mozzarella, ricotta, and salt.

Follow package directions for phyllo to keep it from drying out too quickly. Place a sheet of parchment paper on a baking sheet. Lay one sheet of phyllo on the parchment and brush with melted butter. Repeat with remaining phyllo.

Facing one short end of the phyllo, carefully spread about ⅓ cup mostarda across the center of the rectangle in a strip about 3 inches wide, leaving an inch of pastry clear on either side. Spoon the cheese filling over the mostarda. Fold in the sides of the phyllo against the filling, then bring the bottom third up over the filling. Bring down the top third, loosely tucking the edge under the strudel and making sure the sides are tucked in well. Flip the strudel so the package is mostarda-side up.

Brush with butter and sprinkle with Parmesan cheese. With a serrated knife, cut three slashes across the top of the strudel. Bake for 20 to 25 minutes, until strudel is golden brown. Pull parchment paper with strudel onto a wire rack to cool for 10 minutes, then transfer to a cutting board and slice with a serrated knife into 4 pieces. ◇

GOOD MEDICINE LETTUCE WRAPS

Rhubarb, a native of China, first was employed as a medicinal treatment there, finding wider use as a food when it was brought to Europe by returning explorers. This recipe brings it back to its roots in a variation on the popular Asian lettuce wraps. Morsels of rhubarb lend tartness to this healthful and savory finger food. **SERVES 4.**

SAUCE:

3 tablespoons hoisin sauce

2 tablespoons rice vinegar

1 tablespoon soy or teriyaki sauce

1 teaspoon minced fresh ginger

1 clove garlic, finely minced

1 teaspoon sugar

1 teaspoon sesame oil

½ teaspoon dry mustard

Mix all ingredients together. Set aside to let flavors meld.

FILLING:

- 1 tablespoon canola oil
- 1–2 cloves garlic, minced
- 2 teaspoons freshly grated ginger
- 1 pound ground turkey
- ¾ cup chopped rhubarb
- ⅓ cup chopped salted peanuts
- ¾ cup chopped cucumber
- 1 medium carrot, coarsely grated
- 12 butter, Boston, or iceberg lettuce leaves

....

Heat oil in large saucepan over medium heat and add garlic and ginger. Stir 1 minute, then add turkey, breaking it up as it cooks until it's no longer pink, about 15 minutes. Add sauce and stir to combine, then add rhubarb and cook another 5 minutes. Remove from heat and stir in peanuts, cucumber, and carrot. Serve immediately, letting each person spoon the turkey mixture into the lettuce leaves. ◇

Spicy Chicken Breasts with Creamy Rhubarb Sauce

Serve this piquant, low-fat entrée with couscous or rice, which absorbs every bit of the flavorful sauce. You can use boneless or bone-in chicken breasts. **SERVES 4.**

....

SPICE PASTE:

1 tablespoon sweet paprika

2 teaspoons dried oregano

½ teaspoon salt

2 teaspoons chile paste or ½ teaspoon cayenne pepper

1 tablespoon olive oil

CHICKEN:

1 tablespoon canola oil

4 (6- to 7-ounce) skinless chicken breasts

1 medium onion, chopped (about ¾ cup)

2 cups rhubarb, cut in 1-inch pieces

¼ cup dry vermouth or white wine

½ cup chicken broth

¼ cup crumbled goat cheese, plus more for garnish

⅓ cup chopped parsley

....

In a small bowl, mix together the paste ingredients and set aside.

In a heavy saucepan with a lid, heat oil over medium heat. Place chicken breasts top down in the pan and cook until golden, about 7 to 10 minutes. Turn over and spread spice paste equally over each breast.

Add onion and rhubarb to the pan, in and around the chicken. Add vermouth or white wine and let boil for a minute, then add chicken broth. Reduce heat to low and cook, covered, for 15 minutes. Turn chicken over, spice-side down, cover again, and cook for another 10 minutes. Meanwhile, warm a platter in a 200-degree oven.

Remove chicken to heated platter, spice-side up. Add goat cheese to pan and increase heat, stirring gently to break down onions and rhubarb, about a minute. Stir in parsley. Remove from heat and pour sauce over chicken. Offer additional goat cheese to crumble over chicken, if desired. ◊

Turkey Tenderloins with RhubarBQ Sauce

A short brine period keeps these lean tenderloins tender and juicy on the grill. Baste them in the last five minutes of grilling, but be sure to save back some sauce in the kitchen to heat and serve at the table. **SERVES 8–10.**

....

BRINE:

¼ cup salt

¼ cup sugar

1 gallon water

4 turkey tenderloins (about 2½ pounds)

....

Stir salt and sugar into water until dissolved, then add tenderloins. Cover and refrigerate for 2 hours, no longer, and then remove tenderloins from brine and keep refrigerated until it's time to grill. Prepare RhubarBQ Sauce.

Heat grill to medium-high. Place tenderloins on the grill and roast for 7 to 9 minutes on each side. Check the internal temperature with a meat thermometer. When the tenderloins reach 140 degrees, baste with RhubarBQ Sauce and continue roasting until the temperature is 165 degrees. Remove tenderloins from the grill onto a platter; cover and let sit for 5 minutes so the juices rest. Slice and serve with additional sauce.

If broiling indoors, place the tenderloins on a broiler pan and cook 4 inches from heat, turning once, for 20 to 22 minutes, using the same temperature guidelines for basting and doneness.

RHUBARBQ SAUCE:

   1 tablespoon canola oil

 ½ cup finely chopped yellow onion

 ¾ cup full-flavored beer (like Summit Porter)

   2 cups rhubarb, cut in half-inch pieces

 ½ cup tomato ketchup or Rhubarb Ketchup (page 29)

 ½ cup packed light brown sugar

   2 tablespoons cider vinegar

   1 tablespoon dry mustard

   1 teaspoon dried ginger

   1 teaspoon pomegranate molasses

 ½ teaspoon salt

....

Heat oil in medium saucepan and add onions, stirring to coat. Cover and cook on medium-low heat for 5 minutes, until onions soften. Add beer and bring to a boil. Add rhubarb, and simmer for 5 minutes. Stir in remaining ingredients and continue to simmer for 10 minutes more, stirring often to break down rhubarb. Remove from heat, let cool, and then refrigerate until ready to use. Will keep for 1 week in the refrigerator. ◊

SALMON AND RHUBARB IN PARCHMENT PACKETS

Parchment packages are just plain fun, but they also result in amazingly moist fish. Open the packets at the table to get a burst of aroma as well as to provide a bit of showmanship. You could also substitute any firm white fish for the salmon. A good accompaniment is a rice pilaf garnished with toasted almonds. **SERVES 4.**

....

4 (4-ounce) salmon fillets

salt and pepper, to taste

¼ cup sour cream

¼ cup light mayonnaise

1 teaspoon freshly grated orange zest

4 sheets parchment paper, each 15 inches square

12 asparagus stalks, no thicker than a little finger

⅔ cup finely chopped rhubarb

¼ cup finely sliced scallions, white and some green parts

....

Preheat oven to 400 degrees. Pat the fillets dry and season with salt and pepper. In a small bowl, mix together the sour cream, mayonnaise, and orange zest.

Fold each parchment sheet in half, then open up and lay flat on the counter. On one half of each paper, place three asparagus stalks, then top with a fillet, skin-side down (if there is skin). Divide the sour cream mixture among the fillets, spreading evenly over the surface of the fish. Then sprinkle each fillet with the rhubarb and scallion pieces, dividing evenly.

Fold the parchment paper over the fillet, then tightly pleat the edges closed, folding them twice to create a seal. Place packets on a baking sheet and bake for 15 minutes.

Place each packet on a serving plate and bring to the table. Let each diner cut open the packet with a knife or scissors. ◇

SPICED RHUBARB-SQUASH RAVIOLI

Here's a great way to bring a bit of summer flavor into your winter menu. Pair your favorite winter squash, such as butternut or kabocha, with the rhubarb in your freezer—or your grocer's freezer case. The spicy, creamy filling makes a heavy sauce unnecessary, so these ravioli are best dressed with a drizzle of browned butter and a few crumbles of goat cheese. **MAKES 36 RAVIOLI, TO SERVE 6.**

....

1 medium-sized winter squash (about 3½ pounds)

¼ cup real maple syrup

1 tablespoon soy sauce

½ teaspoon cumin

½ teaspoon cinnamon

1 teaspoon salt, divided

¼ teaspoon nutmeg

5 tablespoons unsalted butter, divided

½ cup finely chopped yellow onion

1 cup rhubarb, cut in half-inch pieces

1 tablespoon sugar

2 (12-ounce [36 count]) packages potsticker wrappers (see note, below)

½ cup crumbled goat cheese

freshly ground pepper

....

Preheat oven to 400 degrees. Coat a rimmed baking sheet well with cooking spray. Cut the squash in half, scoop out the seeds, then cut into slices about 1 inch thick. Mix together syrup, soy sauce, cumin, cinnamon, ½ teaspoon salt, and nutmeg in a large bowl. Dip each side of the squash slices in the mixture and then place in a single layer in the prepared pan. Drizzle with any extra mixture. Bake for 20 minutes, then flip slices. Reduce heat to 350 degrees and bake until tender, about 20 minutes more.

While the squash is baking, melt 1 tablespoon butter in a small saucepan, then add onion and cook over medium-low heat, stirring well until it begins to color. Add rhubarb, sugar, and the remaining ½ teaspoon salt and continue cooking until the onions and rhubarb are soft, stirring to break them down. Remove from heat and set aside.

When the squash is done, peel or cut away the skin from each slice and mash the squash until smooth. Stir in rhubarb-onion mixture and set aside to cool.

Arrange potsticker wrappers across a counter. In the center of each place one rounded tablespoon of filling. Brush edges of each wrapper with water and top with another wrapper, sealing well. Bring a large pot of water to a rolling boil.

While the water is heating, melt the remaining 4 tablespoons butter in a small saucepan over low heat until it begins to turn light brown, separating into liquids and solids. Don't let it scorch. Pour melted butter into small bowl and set aside. Warm a serving bowl in a 200-degree oven.

Add a hefty pinch of salt to the boiling water, then gently add half the ravioli to the pot. Cook until they rise to the surface. Remove from water with slotted spoon and place in preheated bowl. Repeat with remaining ravioli. Drizzle with browned butter, and top with crumbled goat cheese and a few twists from a pepper mill.

Notes: Potsticker wrappers are great for ravioli and cut prep time. But by all means, use fresh pasta from a specialty store or your own recipe for authentic ravioli.

You can freeze the ravioli: place them in a single layer on parchment paper and freeze until solid, then seal in a bag for up to two months. Cook directly from the freezer. ◊

Pork Loin Chops with Rhubarb Stuffing

Rhubarb takes the place of celery in the bread stuffing for this satisfying supper. You can use boneless or bone-in pork chops. **SERVES 4.**

- 1 tablespoon canola oil
- 1½ teaspoons dried thyme, divided
- 1½ teaspoons salt, divided
- ¼ teaspoon pepper
- 4 boneless pork loin chops, ¾ inch thick (about 1½ pounds)
- 3 cups bread, preferably sourdough, cut in half-inch cubes
- 2 cups rhubarb, cut in half-inch pieces
- ½ cup packed light brown sugar
- ¼ cup finely chopped red onion
- 2 tablespoons flour
- ¼ teaspoon allspice

Preheat oven to 350 degrees. In a large saucepan, heat oil. Mix together 1 teaspoon thyme, ½ teaspoon salt, and pepper and sprinkle evenly over chops. Brown chops in oil, about 5 minutes per side.

While chops are browning, combine remaining ingredients, including the remaining ½ teaspoon thyme and 1 teaspoon salt, in a large bowl, tossing well.

When chops are just browned, spread one-third of the rhubarb mixture in the bottom of a 9x9–inch pan coated with cooking spray, then arrange pork chops on top. Cover with remaining rhubarb mixture. Cover pan with foil and bake for 20 minutes. Remove foil and bake for 15 minutes more. ◇

Chop-Chop Sweet and Sour Stir-fry

Our family likes to make this with chicken, but you also can substitute shrimp in this summery stir-fry. **SERVES 4.**

2 leeks

1 bunch kale, preferably Lacinato

2 teaspoons cornstarch

¼ cup water

¼ cup orange juice

3 tablespoons rice vinegar

3 tablespoons sugar

1 tablespoon soy sauce

1 teaspoon Worcestershire sauce

2 tablespoons canola oil

1 inch fresh ginger, peeled and minced

2 large skinless, boneless chicken breasts (about ¾ pound), cut in 1-inch pieces

2 cups rhubarb, cut in 1-inch pieces

rice for serving

Slice leeks into ¼-inch pieces, then rinse thoroughly, separating them into rings and drying on paper towels. Remove center rib from kale leaves; tear leaves into 2-inch pieces to make 2 cups, gently packed.

In a small bowl, combine next 7 ingredients (cornstarch through Worcestershire) and mix well.

In a wok or heavy skillet, heat canola oil until hot. Add ginger and fry about 15 seconds, then add chicken and stir-fry until no longer pink when pierced with a knife. Add rhubarb and leeks and stir-fry for 2 minutes, then add kale.

Add sauce and stir until mixture thickens. Reduce heat and let simmer for about 5 minutes. Serve over rice. ◇

Rhubarb Khoresh

Rhubarb, valued for centuries in China, eventually was exported, but the cost of transport across Asia made it as valuable as saffron and cinnamon. This traditional Persian stew, containing both rhubarb and saffron, must have been a staple of festive occasions.

The rhubarb cooks away to a sauce, which is complemented by a finishing touch of preserved lemon. Serve over basmati rice and pass a bowl of plain yogurt for guests to spoon on top. **SERVES 6.**

- 4 tablespoons butter, divided
- 3 tablespoons olive oil, divided
- 2 large yellow onions, halved and finely sliced
- 2 pounds boneless lamb, shoulder or leg, trimmed of fat and gristle to yield 1½ pounds meat, cut in 1-inch cubes
- 2 generous pinches saffron
- ¼ cup very hot water
- 1 cup finely chopped flat leaf parsley
- ¼ cup finely chopped mint leaves
- 2 cups low-sodium chicken stock
- juice of 1 lemon (about 3 tablespoons)
- 4 cups rhubarb, cut in 2-inch pieces
- 1 teaspoon salt, to taste
- several grinds pepper, to taste
- 1–2 preserved lemon quarters, finely chopped, to taste (recipe follows)
- basmati rice for serving
- plain yogurt for garnish

>>

Melt 3 tablespoons butter with 1 tablespoon oil in a large pan and stir in the onions. Cover and cook over low heat, stirring occasionally, for 15 to 20 minutes, until onions are soft and translucent and barely colored. Scrape into a bowl and set aside.

Add remaining 2 tablespoons olive oil and 1 tablespoon butter to the pan and brown the lamb in three batches so that the pieces are not crowded. When the last batch has browned, return meat and onions to the pan.

Soften the saffron in the hot water for a few minutes, then add saffron-water mixture, herbs, chicken stock, and lemon juice to the meat and onions. Bring to a boil, then cover and reduce heat, simmering for an hour.

Stir in the rhubarb and cook, covered, for another 30 minutes, until the rhubarb breaks down. Season with salt and pepper. Uncover the stew and bring to a low boil to concentrate the juices, stirring to further break down the rhubarb. At the last moment, stir in 1 finely chopped preserved lemon quarter, adding a second quarter if desired.

Serve over rice, with a dollop of yogurt.

Quick Preserved Lemons: If you don't have preserved lemons on hand, you can make this easy substitute. Wash and quarter a lemon, removing seeds. Combine 1 cup water, 1 tablespoon kosher salt, 2 whole cloves, and 1 bay leaf in a small saucepan and bring to a boil. Add lemon quarters to pan. Reduce heat and simmer for 30 minutes, until liquid is reduced and lemon rind is tender. Set aside and cool to room temperature. Remove the bay leaf, and store the remaining half lemon in its cooking liquid in the refrigerator for up to 2 weeks. ◇

PORK MORNINGSIDE

Our neighborhood is called Morningside, so it seemed appropriate to name this variation on Beef Wellington for its origins. This entrée looks impressive, but it's easy, thanks to purchased frozen puff pastry. The layer of ham helps keeps the pastry crisp. **SERVES 4.**

Foundation Recipe for Savory Roasted Rhubarb (page 12)

1 tablespoon canola oil

1 pork tenderloin (about 1½ pounds)

salt and pepper, to taste

1 sheet puff pastry, from 17.3-ounce package, thawed according to package directions

3 slices deli ham

1 egg, beaten

Prepare rhubarb, then increase oven temperature to 400 degrees.

Heat oil in a heavy saucepan. Dry tenderloin with paper towels, then season with salt and pepper. Sear until brown on all sides. Remove from pan and set aside.

Lay a piece of parchment paper on a baking sheet. Unfold pastry onto parchment paper. (Rewrap remaining pastry in plastic wrap and use within 2 days, say, to make 4 of the rhubarb turnovers on page 84.)

>>

Lay ham slices across center of pastry, overlapping, leaving 1 inch of pastry free at each end. Spread rhubarb mixture over ham. Lay pork on top of the rhubarb. Bring up one side of the pastry and drape over the pork, then repeat with the other side. Press to seal. Carefully roll this over so the seam is on the bottom. Pinch together pastry ends and tuck under the roll. Brush the pastry with beaten egg.

Place in oven for 5 minutes, then reduce heat to 350 degrees and bake for 20 minutes, or until meat thermometer inserted in the tenderloin registers 140 degrees. Let the tenderloin rest, uncovered, for 5 minutes before slicing. ◊

DESSERTS

Okay, finally: dessert. But here, too, rhubarb is only too willing to be tweaked and nudged into new flavor combinations. Desserts also are where rhubarb's color variations more often need to be dealt with: no one wants a greenish tart. Depending on the variety, some dishes may need a few drops of red food gel to bring up the color. Others gain their alluring blush from strawberries or raspberries. Frozen rhubarb seems to consistently feature varieties with the reddest stalks, so if faced with too much fresh rhubarb of a greener cast, swap in some from the freezer case.

Most of these recipes err on the tart side. We are eating rhubarb here! But if you have more of a sweet tooth, or if the particular variety you grow or buy at the farmer's market or store is a real pucker fest, you can boost the sweetener to taste in any of these recipes. But take it easy. Let rhubarb be rhubarb.

Rhubarb Pudding Cake

This one is a variation on the "magic" cakes that emerge from the oven cakey and saucy at once, all from pouring boiling water over the batter. SERVES 8–10.

....

- 5 cups rhubarb, cut in half-inch pieces
- 2 cups flour
- ¾ cup packed brown sugar
- 2 teaspoons baking powder
- ½ teaspoon salt

6 tablespoons unsalted butter, melted

²⁄₃ cup milk

1 egg, beaten

1 teaspoon vanilla

¾ cup granulated sugar

1 tablespoon cornstarch

½ teaspoon ground cardamom

1 teaspoon freshly grated lemon zest

1¼ cups boiling water

....

Preheat oven to 350 degrees. Coat a 13x9–inch cake pan with cooking spray. Spread the rhubarb evenly in the pan.

In a large bowl, whisk together flour, brown sugar, baking powder, and salt. By hand or using an electric mixer, beat in the melted butter, milk, egg, and vanilla. The batter will be quite thick. Drop batter in spoonfuls over the rhubarb, then gently spread it to the edges of the pan, covering the rhubarb as much as possible.

In a small bowl, whisk together the sugar, cornstarch, cardamom, and lemon zest. Sprinkle over the batter in an even layer. Gently pour boiling water over the whole mixture.

Bake for 50 minutes. Let cool on wire rack for about 20 minutes. Serve warm with a scoop of ice cream. ◇

Rhubarb-Basil Cornmeal Cakes

These tender cylinders of sponge cake have the slight crunch of cornmeal. The basil may seem an unexpected dessert ingredient but pairs well with the rhubarb for a less-sweet finale to a summer meal. These cakes are best served slightly warm. **SERVES 4.**

3 large eggs, separated

½ teaspoon cream of tartar

⅓ cup sugar

2 tablespoons honey

8 large leaves fresh basil, sliced in thin shreds (about 1 heaping tablespoon), plus smaller leaves for garnish

½ cup cake flour

⅓ cup fine-ground cornmeal

2 tablespoons butter, melted

2 cups rhubarb, cut in half-inch pieces

Rhubarb Glaze (recipe follows)

whipped cream for garnish

Preheat oven to 350 degrees. Thoroughly coat bottoms and sides of four (10-ounce) custard or soufflé cups with cooking spray and place on a baking sheet.

In the large bowl of an electric mixer, beat egg whites with cream of tartar until frothy, then gradually add sugar and beat until the whites hold soft peaks. Set aside.

Heat honey in a microwaveable cup until just boiling. Carefully set aside.

Using an electric mixer, beat egg yolks until the color lightens to pale yellow and they look frothy. Add honey and mix on high speed until yolks almost double in volume. Add basil and mix for 30 seconds.

Whisk together the flour and cornmeal, then fold into yolk mixture. Fold in the melted butter, then gently fold in the egg whites until well combined. Fold in rhubarb.

Divide mixture evenly among baking dishes. Bake for 20 to 25 minutes, or until a wooden pick comes out clean. Remove from the oven and let sit for about 2 minutes. Run a sharp knife around the edge of each cake, then invert, shaking gently if necessary, until cake releases from the pan. If not serving immediately, return cakes to cups.

Drizzle each serving plate with Rhubarb Glaze and serve cakes with a dollop of whipped cream and garnished with a sprig of basil.

Rhubarb Glaze: In a saucepan, combine 2 cups chopped rhubarb with ½ cup water. Bring to a boil, cover, and reduce heat to a simmer for 8 to 10 minutes. Strain mixture and measure out ¾ cup rhubarb liquid; discard solids. Add a few drops of red food gel. In a medium bowl, soften 1 envelope unflavored gelatin in ¼ cup cold water. Return rhubarb liquid to saucepan with ¼ cup sugar and heat to boiling. Pour over gelatin and stir until dissolved. The glaze will thicken slightly as it cools. ◊

RHUBARB CUSTARD PIE

This is Ihla Ode's recipe. She's my mother, which means it was her mother Letha Torkelson's recipe, which means that it's probably similar to recipes in dozens of recipe boxes nurtured by a generation who grew up in a time when rhubarb was more naturally referred to as pie plant. **SERVES 6–8.**

pastry for double-crust pie

1–1½ cups sugar, to taste

2 tablespoons flour

1 teaspoon cinnamon

4 cups rhubarb, cut in half-inch pieces

2 eggs, beaten

1 teaspoon sugar

Preheat oven to 400 degrees. Place bottom crust in pie pan. Whisk together sugar, flour, and cinnamon. Toss together with rhubarb until fruit is evenly coated. Place in prepared pie crust. Top with second crust, crimp the edges closed, and make several decorative cuts in the pastry.

Or, for the classic effect, cut the pastry for the top crust in inch-wide strips and weave them in a lattice pattern. Start by crossing two strips across the filling, then add additional strips one by one, carefully lifting strips and sliding a new strip under them until you reach the edges. Crimp the edges closed.

Pour the beaten eggs evenly over the crust and through the cuts or lattice, then sprinkle with a teaspoon of sugar. Place pie pan on baking sheet. Bake for 10 minutes, then reduce heat to 350 degrees and bake another 30 minutes, or until crust is golden. ◊

SALTED CARAMEL RHUBAPPLE PIE

My daughter, Mimi, came up with the idea for this pie, thinking to blend one of her favorite flavor combinations with my need for a new rhubarb recipe. She was spot-on. A bit of salt in the caramel is a final touch. **SERVES 6–8.**

....

pastry for single-crust pie

⅓ cup walnut pieces

6 Granny Smith apples (about 2¼ pounds), peeled, cored, and thickly sliced

1 tablespoon lemon juice

1 teaspoon cinnamon

1 tablespoon unsalted butter

½ cup honey

½ cup packed brown sugar

2 cups rhubarb, cut in 1-inch pieces

¼ cup instant tapioca

½ teaspoon kosher or sea salt

STREUSEL TOPPING:

½ cup flour

½ cup packed brown sugar

4 tablespoons cold butter, cut in small cubes

Line a pie plate with crust and place in refrigerator while you prepare the filling. Preheat oven to 375 degrees. Spread walnuts on a baking sheet and toast in oven about 5 minutes, until there's a warm, nutty aroma. Cool, then chop coarsely and set aside.

Toss apples with lemon juice and cinnamon. Set aside.

Melt 1 tablespoon butter with honey and ½ cup brown sugar in a large heavy saucepan and heat, stirring constantly, until mixture comes to a rolling boil. Add apples, stirring to coat them with caramel. Reduce heat and cook uncovered no more than 5 minutes. Do not overcook them to mushiness.

Place rhubarb in a bowl. Using a slotted spoon, transfer the hot apples into the bowl with the rhubarb. Add tapioca and stir to combine. Let sit for 15 minutes. In the meantime, add salt to the caramel remaining in the pan and cook, stirring often, a few minutes more to reduce it to a thick syrup. Do not let it scorch. Remove from heat and set aside.

Combine streusel ingredients (flour, sugar, and butter), pinching the butter with your fingers until it's evenly distributed. Stir in the toasted walnuts.

Scrape the apple-rhubarb mixture into the chilled pie shell and drizzle with 3 tablespoons of caramel. Spread streusel mixture over pie and bake for 30 minutes. Let cool on wire rack at least 30 minutes.

Just before serving, drizzle the remaining caramel (reheating if necessary) over the pie. ◇

Strawberry-Rhubarb Pie

The biggest challenge of baking with rhubarb is finding a way to convert all the juiciness into a syrup instead of letting it ooze onto the floor of your oven. Instant tapioca works wonders, especially when pairing these two super-juicy fruits. Balsamic vinegar is the surprise ingredient; its affinity for strawberries also deepens the rhubarb's tartness. **SERVES 6–8.**

4 cups rhubarb, cut in half-inch pieces

3 cups strawberries, hulled and sliced in half-inch pieces

½ cup granulated sugar

¼ cup packed brown sugar

1 tablespoon balsamic vinegar

¼ teaspoon salt

¼ cup instant tapioca

pastry for double-crust pie

1 egg, beaten

sugar for sprinkling

Preheat oven to 400 degrees. In a large bowl, mix together the rhubarb, strawberries, granulated sugar, brown sugar, vinegar, salt, and tapioca. Let sit for 15 minutes.

Place bottom pie crust in pie plate, and pour filling into the prepared pastry. You can place the top crust whole over the pie and crimp to seal. But because this filling has such a gorgeous color, I like to make cut-outs from the top crust—circles, stars, squares, whatever—and arrange them over the filling, almost with as much coverage as a solid crust, but letting the filling peek through. (It's also easier than weaving a lattice.)

Place the pie plate on a baking sheet to catch any drips. Brush crust with beaten egg and sprinkle with a teaspoon of sugar. Bake for 20 minutes, then reduce heat to 350 degrees and bake for about 30 minutes more, until golden. ◊

Frozen Roasted Rhubarb Meringue Pie

This pie is the perfect way to end a warm summer evening, with the pure flavor of rhubarb folded into a frozen meringue. **SERVES 6–8.**

....

GRAHAM CRACKER CRUST:

1¾ cups finely crushed graham crackers (12 large crackers)

¼ cup confectioners' sugar

2 tablespoons butter, melted

2 tablespoons milk

....

Preheat oven to 350 degrees. Lightly coat a pie plate with cooking spray. Stir together cracker crumbs, sugar, butter, and milk until well combined. Reserving 1 tablespoon of crumbs for garnish, press the rest into the pie plate, creating an even layer across the bottom and up the sides. Bake for 15 minutes, then let cool on a wire rack.

FILLING:

Foundation Recipe for Sweet Roasted Rhubarb (page 11)

1 tablespoon Triple Sec liqueur or orange juice

pinch salt

2 large egg whites

½ cup sugar

½ teaspoon cream of tartar

Roast rhubarb and then puree in a blender with Triple Sec or orange juice and salt. Set aside.

Bring about 2 inches of water to a boil in a saucepan over which a medium bowl will fit. While the water is heating, combine egg whites, sugar, and cream of tartar in a medium bowl. Reduce heat to keep the water at a simmer and place the bowl over the saucepan. With a hand-held mixer on medium speed, beat the whites until foamy, about 3 minutes. Increase speed to high and beat until the whites begin to appear glossy, moving the beaters around the bowl, about 3 minutes more. Remove bowl from the pan and set on a counter; continue beating mixture until the meringue holds a stiff peak when the beaters are lifted.

Fold the rhubarb puree into the warm meringue, then scrape into the graham cracker crust. Sprinkle the reserved crumbs over the filling. Place in the freezer, uncovered, for an hour, then gently cover with plastic wrap and freeze until solid, at least 6 hours or preferably overnight. Remove from freezer about 10 minutes before serving to make slicing easier. ◇

Rhubarb Crisp

Call them crisps, crumbles, or simply comfort food, digging into a bowlful of warm fruit and crunchy, caramelized oatmeal topped with a scoop of ice cream or frozen yogurt is one of life's great moments. Okay, maybe it's just a nice moment, but we shouldn't underestimate those, either. Did I mention having this combination for breakfast? Ah, back to a great moment.
SERVES 9.

4 cups rhubarb, cut in 1-inch pieces

1 cup plus 2 tablespoons flour, divided

½ cup granulated sugar

1 teaspoon cinnamon

1 cup packed brown sugar

1 cup old-fashioned (not quick-cooking) oats

pinch salt

8 tablespoons (1 stick) butter, at room temperature

Preheat oven to 350 degrees. Toss rhubarb with 2 tablespoons flour and granulated sugar, then spread evenly in an ungreased 9x9–inch pan. In a medium bowl, mix remaining 1 cup flour, cinnamon, brown sugar, oats, and salt, and then work in the butter with your fingers until the mixture looks crumbly. Spread over the rhubarb and bake for 45 minutes. ◊

RHUBARB CURD

Like the more traditional lemon curd, this rhubarb variation can be used in a variety of ways. It's great on warm scones or toast or dolloped alongside a slice of angel food cake or on a bowlful of fresh strawberries. But if you want to fuss a bit, it's fabulous spread between crepes for a stacked cake or used to fill bite-size rhubarb tassies. Those recipes follow. **MAKES ABOUT 1½ CUPS.**

2½ cups rhubarb, cut in half-inch pieces
⅓ cup plus ½ cup sugar, divided
⅓ cup cranberry juice
4 egg yolks
pinch salt
2 tablespoons unsalted butter, cut in four pieces

Combine rhubarb, ⅓ cup sugar, and cranberry juice in a saucepan and cook over medium heat, stirring frequently, until rhubarb breaks down into a sauce, about 10 minutes. Set aside.

Bring about 2 inches of water to a boil in a saucepan over which a medium bowl will fit. While the water is heating, whisk together the egg yolks, remaining ½ cup sugar, and salt in a medium bowl. Reduce heat to keep the water at a simmer and place the bowl over the saucepan, whisking constantly until the yolk mixture begins to thicken.

When the yolks are quite warm, whisk in the rhubarb mixture, stirring constantly until the mixture thickens. Add the butter a piece at a time, mixing well, then set aside to cool. Refrigerate for up to a week. ◇

RHUBARB CREPE CAKE

A mille crepe is a French "cake" made by layering a filling between crepes (although not the thousand layers of its name). Here, rhubarb curd is spread between 10 to 12 crepes for a make-ahead dessert. The crepes and curd can even be prepared the day before, making party-day assembly a breeze. **SERVES 12.**

....

1½ cups flour

3 tablespoons sugar

1 cup milk

3 large eggs

2 tablespoons unsalted butter, melted, plus additional for crepe pan

1 tablespoon poppy seeds

2 teaspoons freshly grated orange zest

1 teaspoon orange flower water, or vanilla

¼ teaspoon salt

1 recipe Rhubarb Curd (page 69)

   confectioners' sugar

....

Combine first 9 ingredients (flour through salt) in a blender and process until smooth. Pour into bowl, cover, and let rest at room temperature for 30 minutes. You can also refrigerate the batter overnight.

Heat a crepe pan or a small, flat skillet over medium heat, brush with a bit of melted butter, and pour about a quarter cup of batter in the pan, tilting and swirling to make a crepe of even thickness. When the underside of the crepe begins to color, in less than a minute, flip it over with a spatula or your fingers and let cook until the other side begins to color, about 30 seconds. Remove to a clean towel laid over a wire cooling rack and cover. Repeat with remaining batter, stacking the crepes and covering them. Add more butter to the pan as needed.

To make crepe cake, set aside the prettiest crepe for the top. Place one of the other crepes on a serving dish and spread a thin layer of curd, about 2 tablespoons, to the edges. Top with another crepe and repeat until the curd is used up, topping the cake with the prettiest crepe. Cover with plastic wrap and refrigerate for at least 1 hour and up to 6. Sprinkle with confectioners' sugar and cut into wedges with a serrated knife. ◊

RHUBARB MERINGUE TASSIES

These bite-size treats need to be baked the same day you plan to serve them, although the curd and dough can be made several days ahead of time. The results provide a perfect exclamation point to a summer meal on the porch. You'll need a mini-muffin pan for these cookies. **MAKES 24 COOKIES.**

CRUST:

1¼ cups flour

1 tablespoon sugar

pinch salt

8 tablespoons (1 stick) cold unsalted butter, cut in small pieces

4 ounces cold cream cheese, cut in small pieces

1 recipe Rhubarb Curd (page 69)

In a large bowl, whisk together the flour, sugar, and salt. With a pastry blender or your fingers, work the butter into the flour until the butter is evenly distributed in pea-sized clumps. Add the cream cheese and continue to mix the dough until it begins to come together in a mass. Knead in the bowl, squeezing and pressing until you have a ball of dough. Turn out onto a counter and press into a thick disk. Wrap in plastic wrap and refrigerate for at least an hour and up to 2 days.

To make the tassies, preheat the oven to 350 degrees. Remove the dough from the refrigerator. Cut or pinch off a piece of dough about the size of a large grape and roll it into a ball. Press the dough into a mini-muffin cup, making sure the bottom isn't too thin and shaping the sides so they're level with the pan. Fill each cup with about 1 teaspoon rhubarb curd. Bake for 15 to 20 minutes, or until the pastry is golden and firm around the edges.

While the tassies are baking, make the meringue.

>>

MERINGUE:

2 egg whites

½ teaspoon cream of tartar

pinch salt

½ cup sugar

¼ teaspoon vanilla

....

In bowl of a standing mixer, beat egg whites, cream of tartar, and salt on medium-high speed until frothy and the beater begins to leave a path. Begin adding sugar one spoonful at a time, slowly but steadily, until meringue holds a stiff peak when beaters are lifted. Add vanilla and mix until just combined.

After the tassies are baked, reduce the oven heat to 325 degrees. Top each warm tassie with a dollop of meringue or use a pastry bag to pipe a swirl onto each cookie. Bake for 10 minutes, or until meringue begins to color and set. Using a fork, carefully lift each tassie and place it on a wire rack to cool. Serve at once, or refrigerate the tassies until serving time. ◇

Orange Sponge Roulade with Rhubarb Filling

Roulades are much easier to make than they look, so with very little effort it will seem like you fussed. Plus, you can't beat the combo of a light sponge cake and tart, creamy filling. **SERVES 10.**

....

CAKE:

- ⅓ cup cake flour
- 3 tablespoons cornstarch
- 2 teaspoons freshly grated orange zest
- 5 large eggs
- ½ cup plus 2 tablespoons granulated sugar, divided
- ¼ teaspoon cream of tartar
- ½ teaspoon vanilla
- ¼ cup confectioners' sugar

....

Preheat oven to 450 degrees. Cut a sheet of parchment paper to lay flat inside a 10x15–inch jelly roll pan. Coat well with cooking spray. In a small bowl, whisk together the flour, cornstarch, and orange zest.

Separate two eggs, placing the yolks in a large mixing bowl and the whites in another large bowl. Separate a third egg, adding the yolk to the yolks and saving or discarding the white. Add the remaining two whole eggs to the yolks. Add ½ cup sugar to yolks. Set aside.

Beat the egg whites and the cream of tartar until foamy, then slowly beat in remaining 2 tablespoons sugar until stiff peaks form when the beater is lifted. Set aside.

Beat the yolk mixture on high speed until the mixture is light and fluffy, about 5 minutes. Mix in vanilla.

>>

Gently spoon the flour mixture over the yolk mixture and fold it in, lifting the batter and folding it over the flour until it's incorporated. Add the whites to the batter and fold them in as well, making sure to lift and fold to keep the whites from deflating, until no streaks remain.

Pour the batter into the prepared pan, smoothing it from edge to edge. Bake for 7 minutes, until the cake springs back when pressed lightly.

While the cake is baking, lay a clean dish towel on the counter and sprinkle evenly with confectioners' sugar. When the cake is done, run a knife around the edges to loosen, then flip the pan over onto the dish towel. Lift off the pan, peel off the parchment paper, and then gently roll up the cake, towel and all, from the long side. This step "teaches" the cake to curve as it cools.

FILLING:

1 cup heavy cream

¼ cup confectioners' sugar, plus more for serving

Foundation Recipe for Sweet Roasted Rhubarb (page 11)

In a medium bowl, beat the cream and confectioners' sugar until stiff. Fold in the roasted rhubarb.

Unroll the cake and spread with rhubarb filling, leaving 1 inch free along the long side. Re-roll—this time without the towel!—then cover with plastic wrap and refrigerate for at least 1 hour and up to 6 hours. Sprinkle with additional confectioners' sugar before slicing to serve. ◊

Rhubarb-Peach Pavlovas

Filled with rosy rhubarb and golden peaches, these individual meringue desserts are like serving little sunrises breaking through the clouds.

SERVES 8.

....

1 cup plus 1 tablespoon sugar, divided

1 tablespoon cornstarch

4 large egg whites, at room temperature

½ teaspoon cream of tartar

1 teaspoon vanilla

Foundation Recipe for Sweet Roasted Rhubarb (page 11)

2–3 large peaches, pitted and chopped

1 cup heavy cream

....

Preheat oven to 300 degrees and place rack in the middle position. Cover baking sheet with parchment paper. In a small bowl, whisk together 1 cup sugar and cornstarch.

In the bowl of a large mixer, combine egg whites and cream of tartar. Beat at medium-high speed until the mixture is white and foamy and the beater leaves a faint trace. Begin adding sugar mixture a spoonful at a time, slowly but steadily, until all the sugar has been added and the whites hold stiff peaks when the beater is lifted. Add the vanilla and beat about 30 seconds on high speed.

Using a large spoon, drop 8 dollops of meringue onto the baking sheet, gently shaping them into nests with a slight depression in the center. Or, place the meringue in a pastry bag fitted with a fluted tip and pipe circles onto the paper, building up the edge to make a "nest."

>>

Place meringues in the oven and immediately reduce heat to 200 degrees. Bake for 1½ hours, then turn off heat and leave meringues in the oven for several hours, until completely cool.

Prepare the roasted rhubarb, then puree in a blender, or simply stir briskly if you prefer more texture. Set aside to cool. Toss peaches with remaining 1 tablespoon sugar to juice a bit. Beat the cream until stiff, then fold in half of the rhubarb.

Place a generous spoonful of rhubarb whipped cream in each meringue, top with peaches, and drizzle with remaining rhubarb puree. Serve immediately. ◇

Rhubarb Foster

Bananas Foster is one of the great desserts, but the creaminess of the bananas and the sweetness of the sugary rum can overwhelm—in a good way, but still. Rhubarb provides a welcome counterpoint of flavor but also a bit of color to this dramatic dessert. **SERVES 8.**

```
  2  eggs
1½  cups flour
 ⅓  cup sugar
 ½  teaspoon baking soda
    pinch salt
  1  teaspoon vanilla
  2  cups milk
```

Combine all ingredients in a blender and whirl until well mixed. Pour into bowl, cover, and set aside for 30 minutes or refrigerate overnight.

Heat a crepe pan or a small, flat skillet over medium heat, brush with a bit of melted butter, and pour about a quarter cup of batter in the pan, tilting and swirling to make a crepe of even thickness. When the underside of the crepe begins to color, in less than a minute, flip it over with a spatula or your fingers and let cook until the other side begins to color, another minute. Remove to a clean towel laid over a wire cooling rack and cover. Repeat with remaining batter, stacking the crepes and covering them. Add more butter to pan as needed. Cooled crepes may be placed in a plastic bag, towel and all, and refrigerated for up to 1 day.

When ready to serve, place two crepes, folded in quarters, in each of 8 bowls and proceed.

>>

BANANA-RHUBARB MIXTURE:

4 tablespoons unsalted butter

1 cup lightly packed dark brown sugar

½ teaspoon cinnamon

2 cups rhubarb, cut in half-inch pieces

4 firm bananas, peeled, halved, and split

¼ cup dark rum

vanilla ice cream

....

In a skillet, melt the butter over medium heat, then stir in the brown sugar and cinnamon and cook, stirring constantly, until sugar has melted. Add the rhubarb, stir to coat, and cook 2 to 3 minutes. Add bananas, rounded-side down, and cook until they begin to soften, 2 to 3 minutes.

Gently turn over the bananas. Remove pan from heat and pour in rum. Return the pan to the burner, increase the heat to high and, with a match at the edge of the pan, carefully ignite the rum. Give the pan a few shakes until the flames go out.

Divide caramelized fruits among the bowls, then serve with a scoop of vanilla ice cream. ◊

Rhubarb Swirlygigs

This recipe has been in our family forever, although Mom always made it with Bisquick. This version returns us to a day before such convenience foods. Crazy, huh? **SERVES 9.**

1 cup plus 3 tablespoons sugar, divided
1 cup water
2½ cups flour
1 tablespoon baking powder
½ teaspoon salt
¼ teaspoon freshly grated nutmeg
1½ cups half-and-half
3 cups rhubarb, cut in half-inch pieces
2 tablespoons butter, cut in small pieces
cream or ice cream

Preheat oven to 425 degrees. Coat a 9x9–inch pan with cooking spray. In a heavy saucepan, bring 1 cup sugar and water to a boil and cook for 5 minutes. Set aside.

In a medium bowl, whisk together flour, baking powder, salt, and nutmeg. Stir in half-and-half until just combined. Turn out onto a lightly floured surface and knead about 15 seconds, until the dough holds together. Pat or roll into a 12-inch square.

Spread rhubarb evenly over the surface, pressing gently and leaving about 1 inch along the top edge. Dot with butter and sprinkle with 2 tablespoons sugar. Gently roll up like a jelly roll, reaching the 1-inch top border and then rocking lightly to seal. Using a serrated knife, cut the roll into 9 equal slices. Lay slices in three rows in the pan, tucking in any pieces of rhubarb that fall out during the transfer. Pour sugar syrup over the spirals and sprinkle with remaining tablespoon sugar.

Bake for 25 to 30 minutes. Serve warm with cream or ice cream. ◊

Rhubarb-Ricotta Turnovers

Vanilla sugar isn't crucial here, but it's wonderful. The aroma alone is tempting, but it also adds a sophisticated layer of flavor to these hand pies.
MAKES 8 LARGE TURNOVERS.

2 cups thinly sliced rhubarb

⅓ cup vanilla sugar or granulated sugar (see headnote)

2 tablespoons cornstarch

½ cup ricotta cheese

1 tablespoon confectioners' sugar

1 teaspoon freshly grated lemon zest

1 (17.3-ounce) package puff pastry, thawed

1 egg, beaten

decorative sugar

ice cream

Preheat oven to 350 degrees. Mix together rhubarb, vanilla sugar, and cornstarch and set aside. Mix together ricotta cheese, confectioners' sugar, and lemon zest. Set aside.

On a floured surface, carefully unfold each sheet of pastry and lay flat. Roll out to a 12-inch square. Cut each square into four equal squares. Place about a tablespoon of ricotta just off center in each square, then spoon a quarter cup of rhubarb evenly over and around the ricotta. Brush the edges of each square with beaten egg, then fold to enclose, using a fork to crimp shut. Brush turnovers with more egg, then sprinkle with decorative sugar. Make one small cut in the crust to release steam.

Bake for 35 to 40 minutes, until golden. Cool on wire rack and then serve with ice cream. ◇

Coconut Crunch Torte
with Rhubarb-Pineapple Filling

This is another recipe I grew up with, and I suspect its origins are with my grandmother's family in Texas. We always served it plain with ice cream, but adding a tart rhubarb compote laced with pineapple is a delight. Yeah, you can still have the ice cream, too. **SERVES 6–8.**

....

1¼ cups finely crushed graham crackers (1 sleeve of crackers)

½ cup shredded sweetened coconut

½ cup chopped walnuts

4 egg whites

¼ teaspoon salt

1 teaspoon vanilla

1 cup sugar

....

Preheat oven to 350 degrees. Thoroughly coat a 9-inch pie plate with cooking spray.

In a small bowl, mix together cracker crumbs, coconut, and nuts. In bowl of a standing mixer, beat the egg whites with salt and vanilla until foamy. Gradually add sugar until the whites keep a stiff peak when the beater is lifted. Fold cracker mixture into the whites, then scrape into pie plate, smoothing mixture and building up the sides. Bake for 30 minutes. While the torte is baking, make the filling.

>>

RHUBARB-PINEAPPLE FILLING:

¾ cup sugar

3 tablespoons cornstarch

1 (8-ounce) can crushed pineapple with juice

1 cup rhubarb, cut in half-inch pieces

1 tablespoon lemon juice

....

In a medium saucepan, combine sugar, cornstarch, pineapple with juice, rhubarb, and lemon juice. Cook over medium heat, stirring constantly until thickened, about 10 minutes. Set aside.

Cool torte on a wire rack. When ready to serve, spread rhubarb filling in the center. Cut in wedges and serve with ice cream or frozen yogurt. ◇

ROASTED RHUBARB-GINGER GRANITA

This cool granita tingles with the tart rhubarb and the subtle heat of ginger. For a refreshing summer dessert cocktail, place a scoop in a goblet and top off with prosecco or champagne. **MAKES 1 PINT.**

- 2 cups water
- 1 cup packed brown sugar
- 1 cinnamon stick
- 1 inch fresh ginger, peeled and grated
- 1 vanilla bean, split in half
- 2 batches Foundation Recipe for Sweet Roasted Rhubarb (page 11)
- 2 tablespoons vodka, optional

Combine water, sugar, cinnamon, ginger, and vanilla bean in a saucepan and bring to a boil. Reduce heat and simmer for 5 minutes. Strain liquid, discarding cinnamon stick and ginger. Dry and save the vanilla bean for another use.

Combine the roasted rhubarb with the sugar syrup. Stir in vodka if desired (the alcohol improves the granita's texture). Pour mixture into a pan and place in the freezer for 2 hours. Remove and stir briskly, breaking up any ice crystals. Cover and return to the freezer until solid, at least 6 hours. ◇

Persian Rhubarb Snack Cake

The depth of flavor in the rhubarb compote comes from pomegranate molasses, increasingly available in most groceries. Combined with pistachios, this moist snack cake is fine on its own or with a dollop of yogurt. **MAKES 2 (9-INCH) LOAF CAKES.**

....

RHUBARB COMPOTE:

2 cups fresh rhubarb, cut in half-inch pieces

3 tablespoons sugar

1 tablespoon pomegranate molasses

freshly grated zest of 1 orange

juice of 1 orange (about ¼ cup)

pinch salt

....

Combine all ingredients in a large saucepan and cook over medium heat, stirring often, until the rhubarb is soft and begins to break down into a sauce. Watch closely; this won't take long. Set aside.

CAKE:

½ cup shelled unsalted pistachios, divided

1¾ cups packed brown sugar, divided

½ teaspoon cinnamon

1 tablespoon unsalted butter, melted

2 cups all-purpose flour

½ cup whole wheat flour

1 teaspoon baking powder

½ teaspoon baking soda

1 teaspoon salt

1 cup buttermilk

½ cup canola oil

1 teaspoon vanilla

1 egg, lightly beaten

....

Preheat oven to 400 degrees, and coat two 9x5–inch loaf pans with cooking spray.

In a small saucepan over medium heat, toast pistachios, stirring frequently, until they grow fragrant and begin to color just a bit, about 5 minutes. Don't let them scorch. Pour nuts out onto a cutting board and chop them up a bit, but not too fine. Measure out 2 tablespoons pistachios and mix together in a small bowl with ¼ cup brown sugar, cinnamon, and melted butter. Set aside.

In a large bowl, whisk together flours, baking powder, baking soda, and salt. Stir in remaining pistachios. Coating the nuts with flour will keep them from sinking to the bottom of the cake.

In a medium bowl, combine remaining 1½ cups brown sugar, buttermilk, oil, vanilla, and egg. Mix well. Add to the dry ingredients and stir until everything is moistened. Add rhubarb compote and stir until well combined. Divide batter between the two pans. Sprinkle cinnamon-nut mixture over the loaves, then place in oven and bake for 10 minutes. Reduce heat to 325 degrees and bake for 30 to 35 minutes, or until a wooden pick inserted in the center of the cake comes out clean.

Let the cakes sit in the pans for about 5 minutes, then gently invert onto a wire cooling rack, turning right-side up again to cool. ◊

SOUR CREAM–RHUBARB TORTE WITH MERINGUE TOPPING

I'm not sure we ever had a July Fourth family reunion without this dessert being somewhere on the groaning board. Every aunt knew how to make it, so they must have decided beforehand whose year it was to bring it. It's a classic. This dessert should be served the same day it's made. **SERVES 9.**

CRUST:

1 cup flour

8 tablespoons (1 stick) cold unsalted butter, cut in small pieces

2 tablespoons sugar

....

Preheat oven to 350 degrees. In a 9x9–inch pan, combine all ingredients, working in the butter with your fingers until evenly distributed. Press the dough in an even layer across the bottom of the pan. Bake for 7 minutes. Cool on wire rack. Leave oven on.

FILLING:

4 egg yolks (save the whites for the meringue)

1 cup sour cream

1 cup sugar

2 tablespoons orange juice

3 cups rhubarb, cut in half-inch pieces

1 tablespoon cornstarch

In a medium bowl, whisk together egg yolks, sour cream, sugar, and orange juice. Toss rhubarb with cornstarch, then stir into sour cream mixture. Pour into the prebaked crust and bake for 50 to 60 minutes, or until the filling appears firm. Set on wire rack. About 15 minutes before the torte is done, start preparing the meringue.

MERINGUE:

8 tablespoons sugar, divided

1 tablespoon cornstarch

½ cup water

4 egg whites

½ teaspoon cream of tartar

½ teaspoon salt

1 teaspoon vanilla

In a small saucepan, combine 2 tablespoons sugar, cornstarch, and water and bring to a boil, cooking until mixture thickens and becomes clear. Remove from heat and set aside.

Using a stand mixer, beat egg whites, cream of tartar, and salt until frothy. Add remaining 6 tablespoons sugar one spoonful at a time, then beat in vanilla. Mixture should not yet hold stiff peaks. Slowly add the warm cornstarch mixture and continue mixing until the meringue holds a stiff peak when the beater is lifted.

Spread the meringue on the warm torte and return to the oven for about 10 minutes, or until the meringue begins to color. Cool completely. Refrigerate until serving. ◈

RHUBARB COBBLER WITH CHEESE BISCUITS

Fruit and cheese make a wonderful dessert combo, as in this not-too-sweet cobbler. Rhubarb pairs especially well with Swiss-type cheeses such as Gruyère, Emmentaler, or Jarlsberg, but a good Wisconsin white Cheddar also would be tasty. **SERVES 12.**

8 cups rhubarb, cut in half-inch pieces

½ cup plus 2 tablespoons granulated sugar, divided

½ cup packed brown sugar

1 tablespoon cornstarch

1 cup cornmeal

1 cup flour

2 teaspoons baking powder

½ teaspoon baking soda

¼ teaspoon salt

4 tablespoons cold unsalted butter, cut in pieces

4 ounces grated cheese (about 1 cup; see headnote)

1 egg, beaten

1 cup buttermilk

Preheat oven to 400 degrees. Toss together the rhubarb, ½ cup granulated sugar, brown sugar, cornstarch, and a pinch of salt, and spread evenly in a 13x9–inch pan.

In a medium bowl, whisk together the cornmeal, flour, remaining 2 tablespoons granulated sugar, baking powder, baking soda, and ¼ teaspoon salt. Using a pastry blender or your fingers, work the butter into the dry ingredients until evenly distributed in pea-sized clumps. Add the cheese and toss until evenly distributed. Stir in beaten egg and buttermilk all at once, mixing until just moistened.

Using an ice cream scoop or a large spoon, arrange 12 dollops of the dough over the rhubarb. Bake for 25 to 30 minutes. Let cool slightly before serving. ◇

Rhubarb Burnt Creams

These individual desserts are super simple but look like works of art. The only trick is watching the sugar syrup carefully; once it turns a rich shade of amber, take it off the heat and start drizzling! If at all possible, use shallow 8-ounce dishes for the best presentation, but custard cups will work, too. **SERVES 8.**

....

3 cups rhubarb, cut in half-inch pieces

2 tablespoons water, divided

1 cup sugar, divided

½ cup heavy cream

1 cup vanilla flavored Greek yogurt

....

In a heavy saucepan, combine rhubarb and 1 tablespoon water and cook over low heat, covered and stirring occasionally, until fruit is tender, about 10 minutes. Begin stirring briskly to break down rhubarb, mashing it against the sides of the pan. Turn up heat and cook until most of the juices evaporate, leaving a thick puree. Add ½ cup sugar and stir until dissolved. Divide the puree among eight dishes and let cool.

In a small bowl, beat the cream until stiff, then gently fold in the yogurt. Spoon over the rhubarb puree and smooth the tops. Freeze for a half hour, until the cream is firm.

Arrange dishes on the counter before you begin to make syrup. Things move fast once the caramel is ready. In a small heavy saucepan, stir together the remaining ½ cup sugar and tablespoon water over low heat. When the sugar is dissolved, increase the heat and watch carefully until the mixture begins to boil and the sugar changes from light golden to medium to a warm golden color. Remove from heat and, working quickly, use a spoon to drizzle the desserts with squiggles of sugar syrup until all the syrup is used. It will harden on contact. Serve immediately or refrigerate and serve within 3 hours. ◊

Rhubarb-Raspberry Clafouti

Clafouti is a little cakey, a little custardy—sweet and fruity under a shower of confectioners' sugar. The rum or brandy is optional but adds another layer of flavor. **SERVES 6.**

....

2 cups chopped rhubarb

1 cup fresh raspberries

⅓ cup confectioners' sugar, plus more for serving

½ teaspoon cinnamon

3 large eggs

½ cup granulated sugar

½ teaspoon salt

1½ cups milk

1 tablespoon rum or brandy

1 teaspoon vanilla

¾ cup flour

....

Preheat oven to 375 degrees. Coat a 10-inch pie plate or other shallow baking dish with cooking spray. Spread rhubarb and raspberries in the bottom of the pan and sprinkle with confectioners' sugar and cinnamon. Bake for 10 minutes and remove from oven.

Combine the eggs, sugar, salt, milk, and flavorings in a blender and process until smooth. Add flour and process until combined. You can also do this with a whisk, a bowl, and some muscle.

Pour batter over the fruit mixture and bake for 20 to 25 minutes, until puffed and golden. Let rest for 15 minutes. Sprinkle with confectioners' sugar, then cut into wedges and serve. ◇

GINGERY RHUBARB UPSIDE-DOWN CAKE

Take a little extra time to arrange the rhubarb in an attractive pattern and take care in spreading the batter. The payoff will be a jewel-like design when the cake is revealed. **SERVES 8.**

....

- 12 tablespoons (1½ sticks) butter, at room temperature, divided
- ½ cup packed light brown sugar
- 2 tablespoons finely chopped crystallized ginger, divided
- 1 teaspoon cinnamon
- 2 cups rhubarb, sliced into 2-inch pieces (or enough to cover the bottom of the pan, depending on the size of the stalks)
- 1½ cups flour
- 2 teaspoons baking powder
- ½ teaspoon salt
- ¾ cup granulated sugar
- 2 eggs
- 1 teaspoon vanilla
- ½ cup half-and-half

....

Preheat oven to 350 degrees and set rack in the middle position. Place 4 tablespoons butter in a 9-inch cake pan and set in oven until butter is melted. Meanwhile, mix together brown sugar, 1 tablespoon ginger, and cinnamon.

Remove pan from oven and stir the brown sugar mixture into the butter, spreading it into an even layer. Arrange the rhubarb pieces, flat-side up, in an attractive design, filling in the gaps with smaller pieces to make a solid layer of fruit.

In a medium bowl, whisk together the flour, baking powder, salt, and remaining tablespoon ginger.

Using a stand mixer, beat the remaining 8 tablespoons butter until smooth, then add the granulated sugar and beat until light and fluffy, about 5 minutes. Don't skimp on this step. Add the eggs and vanilla and beat until smooth. With the mixer set at low speed, add half of the dry ingredients, then a quarter cup of the half-and-half. Repeat with the remaining ingredients.

Spoon the batter in dollops over the rhubarb and smooth the top so no fruit is visible. Bake for 45 to 50 minutes, or until a wooden pick inserted in the center of the cake comes out clean. Let the cake cool for 10 minutes in the pan, then place a serving plate over the cake. Working carefully but confidently, flip over the pan and let it sit until the cake releases onto the plate. This may happen right away or it could take a minute or two. Lift off the cake and rearrange any rhubarb pieces that might have been dislodged. ◊

SAWTOOTH MACAROONS

Use your pinkest stalks here; the little ruby-red nuggets will stand out against the white coconut in this sweet-tart cookie. I like to shape the macaroons into little peaks, which remind me of the Sawtooth Range along Minnesota's North Shore, which also happens to be a prime rhubarb climate. This recipe is adapted from the classic on the Baker's coconut bag.

MAKES ABOUT 3 DOZEN COOKIES.

....

  1 (14-ounce) package flaked sweetened coconut (about 5⅓ cups)

1½ cups rhubarb, cut in quarter-inch cubes

⅓ cup granulated sugar

⅓ cup packed light brown sugar

  6 tablespoons flour

  4 egg whites

¼ teaspoon salt

  1 teaspoon orange flower water, or vanilla

....

Mix together the coconut, rhubarb, sugars, and flour in a large bowl. In another bowl, whisk the egg whites, salt, and orange flower water or vanilla until frothy. Stir into coconut mixture until well blended. Let sit for 10 minutes.

Preheat oven to 350 degrees and set rack in the middle position. Line a baking sheet with parchment paper. Drop coconut mixture by tablespoonfuls onto the baking sheet, pressing together with your fingers to form a peak. Bake for 20 minutes or until golden brown. Pull the parchment paper with the macaroons onto a wire rack to cool completely before carefully peeling away the paper. Macaroons will keep for several days in an airtight container. ◊

BREADS

Rhubarb is a natural in quick breads, lending some color and dash to basic backdrops of flour and sugar, as well as ensuring a moist product.

EASTERN SKY SCONES

In addition to wonderfully melding flavors, pink rhubarb and orange mango make these breakfast treats rival the sunrise. The cardamom lends a hint of Scandinavia. **MAKES 8 SCONES.**

2 cups flour

3 tablespoons sugar

1 tablespoon baking powder

½ teaspoon salt

½ teaspoon ground cardamom

8 tablespoons (1 stick) cold unsalted butter, cut in small pieces

1 cup rhubarb, cut in half-inch pieces

1 cup mango, cut in half-inch pieces

1 cup heavy cream

decorative pearl sugar, optional

Preheat oven to 450 degrees and set rack in the middle position. In a large bowl, whisk together the flour, sugar, baking powder, salt, and cardamom. With a pastry blender or your fingers, work in the butter until it's well distributed and few lumps remain. Stir in the rhubarb and the mango, then add the cream, stirring until just moistened.

Turn mixture out onto a lightly floured surface and knead several times, until the dough holds together. Shape into a 9-inch circle, and cut into eight wedges.

Using a spatula, transfer the wedges to a baking sheet, leaving at least an inch between them. Sprinkle with decorative sugar, if desired, and bake for 13 to 15 minutes, or until light golden brown. Cool briefly on a wire rack, and serve warm. ◇

RHUBARB GRAHAM MUFFINS

Crushed graham crackers give these muffins a subtle new flavor. **MAKES 12 LARGE MUFFINS.**

....

- 1¼ cups finely crushed graham crackers (1 sleeve of crackers)
- 1 cup flour
- ½ cup packed brown sugar
- 1 teaspoon baking powder
- ½ teaspoon baking soda
- ¼ teaspoon salt
- 1 egg, beaten
- ½ cup buttermilk
- ⅓ cup canola oil
- ¾ cup chopped rhubarb
- ⅓ cup shredded sweetened coconut

....

Preheat oven to 375 degrees. Coat muffin cups with cooking spray or line with paper baking cups.

Whisk together cracker crumbs, flour, brown sugar, baking powder, baking soda, and salt. In a small bowl, stir together the egg, buttermilk, and oil. Add to dry ingredients and stir until just moistened. Fold in rhubarb and coconut. Fill muffin cups two-thirds full. Bake for 18 to 20 minutes, until golden. ◊

SAVORY RHUBARB BISCUITS

These biscuits are a tasty addition to any dinner table, and they also have an encore life when filled with leftover ham and good mustard. Next time you make a pot pie, consider these as a topper. As with all biscuits, mix with a light hand and work quickly. Placing them upside-down on the baking sheet helps them rise higher. **MAKES 12–16 BISCUITS**

> 2 cups flour
> 2 teaspoons baking powder
> ½ teaspoon baking soda
> 1 teaspoon salt
> ½ teaspoon freshly ground pepper
> 8 tablespoons (1 stick) cold unsalted butter, cut in half-inch cubes
> 1 shallot, finely minced (about 1 tablespoon)
> ½ cup finely chopped rhubarb
> ½ cup grated Cheddar cheese
> 1 cup buttermilk

Preheat oven to 425 degrees. Mix together flour, baking powder, baking soda, salt, and pepper. Add the chilled butter and cut in with a pastry blender—or use your fingers—until the butter is the size of peas. Stir in the shallot, rhubarb, and cheese and toss until well coated. Stir in buttermilk and mix just until dough is moistened.

Turn the dough out onto a lightly floured surface and knead a bit to bring it together. Pat into a circle about a half-inch thick. With a two-inch cookie cutter, cut out rounds as close together as possible. Place biscuits bottom side-up on baking sheet. Pat the remaining scraps together and cut more biscuits until all the dough is used. Bake for 20 minutes, or until golden. Serve immediately. ◇

Zucchini-Rhubarb Bread

You didn't think we were going to let you out of here without a recipe for zucchini bread, did you? This icon of summer gets a makeover, though, zinged with rhubarb and orange peel. For the best orange flavor, don't use a zester but slice the peel from the orange in strips, cut away any bitter white pith, and mince it into tiny bits. **MAKES 1 (9-INCH) LOAF.**

....

- 1 cup all-purpose flour
- ½ cup whole wheat flour
- 1 cup packed brown sugar
- 2 teaspoons baking powder
- ½ teaspoon ground ginger
- ½ teaspoon baking soda
- ½ teaspoon salt
- 2 eggs
- ⅓ cup canola oil
- 1 cup shredded zucchini
- 1 cup finely chopped rhubarb
- 1 tablespoon chopped orange peel

....

Preheat oven to 375 degrees and coat a 9x5-inch bread pan with cooking spray. Whisk together the flours, sugar, baking powder, ginger, baking soda, and salt. In a medium bowl, beat together the eggs and oil. Stir in the zucchini, rhubarb, and orange peel. Stir in the dry ingredients and mix until no dry spots remain. Scrape into prepared pan.

Bake for 50 to 60 minutes, or until wooden pick inserted in the center of the loaf comes out clean. Cool in the pan for 5 minutes, then invert onto a wire rack to continue cooling. ◊

BEVERAGES

Rhubarb's flavor is ideal for any number of refreshing summer drinks, whether you choose to add alcohol or not. Included here is a recipe for a flavor base and some suggestions for its use. And, of course, a recipe for rhubarb wine, just because.

RHUBARB BASE

This essentially is a rhubarb broth, made simply by simmering rhubarb in just enough water with just enough sugar, then straining out the blush-colored juice. The variations are what your taste buds suggest. To the rhubarb mixture, consider adding a few slices of fresh ginger or a few sprigs of fresh mint or basil. Some may like the bracing herbiness of rosemary, while others may go in the other direction with a vanilla bean.

After that, it's a question of adding a bit of booze or just going for thirst-quenching goodness. Rhubarb's tartness pairs well with sweet dark rum. Adding a jigger of rhubarb base to a classic Dark 'n' Stormy, with its ginger beer and lime, is a natural. But a simple combo of base and icy vodka is tasty, especially with a twist of orange peel.

I explored the world of Rhubarb Bitters—anything for you, dear reader—made by Fee Brothers, a revered bitters manufacturer from Rochester, New York. I remain underwhelmed, but perhaps more research is needed?

In any case, here's where we start:

2 cups rhubarb, cut in 1-inch pieces
2 tablespoons sugar
water
few drops red food gel, optional

Place rhubarb in a medium saucepan with the sugar and add enough water so the rhubarb is just covered. Bring to a boil, then simmer for 30 minutes, stirring occasionally. (Here's where you can experiment by adding herbs, ginger, or other ingredients to the simmering mixture.) If your rhubarb stalks are mostly green, consider adding some food coloring.

Strain through a colander or cheesecloth into a bowl. You should end up with a little more than a cup. The recipe can be easily doubled or tripled. Once all the juice has dripped through, discard the pulp. Resist adding additional sugar unless the juice is super tart. Tartness is what rhubarb is all about.

You can use the rhubarb base in several ways:

◇ Add a 1-ounce jigger to a Dark 'n' Stormy, preferably made with Gosling's brand ingredients: Pour a half can of Gosling's Ginger Beer over ice in a tumbler. Add 1 to 2 ounces Gosling's dark rum, then rhubarb base. Finish with a squeeze of fresh lime.

◇ Serve 2 to 3 parts rhubarb base to 1 part vodka over ice with a twist of orange.

◇ Drop a raspberry in each of two wineglasses, then add a half cup of base to each and top with prosecco or champagne.

◇ Combine 2 to 3 parts rhubarb base with 1 part dark rum and serve over ice with a twist of lime. A few splashes of rhubarb bitters may be in order, but that's up to you.

◇ One recipe rhubarb base added to two quarts of sun tea puts a fruity spin on a summer refresher.

◇ Use the rhubarb base as a substitute in cocktails calling for cranberry juice.

◇ Add some rhubarb base to club soda or lemonade—you're getting the idea! ◇

Rhubarb Wine

I saw you flinch. And it's okay. The idea of rhubarb wine has that effect on people, for reasons both experienced and suspected. I grew up with rhubarb wine being a part of many family gatherings over a South Dakota winter. Thanksgiving was when the drink was first drinkable and, theoretically, it would improve with age throughout the months of blizzards until the new rhubarb told us it was spring.

Rhubarb wine isn't so much about its alcohol content as its sugar levels. It is, as wine aficionados might say, a sweet wine. Dentists may concur. Frankly, we often drank it as a wine spritzer, cut with a little club soda.

I know I sound as if we didn't really enjoy it. And the truth is, enjoy *isn't really the right word. Yet my grandma and my mother and now my sister make rhubarb wine because, well, someone needs to make it. It's part of our rural tradition, part of family gatherings. And every so often, depending on the rhubarb, you can end up with a batch of pretty good wine.*

Here's the recipe as I recorded it when my grandma, Claudina Ode (who lived to be one hundred, so there's that), was still alive:

Start with rhubarb—lots of it. You need to tug so many stalks from the plant that you'll trip over the dog, your arms will be so full. Once you lop off the leaves and that gorgeous pink knob at the root, you'll want to end up with 20 pounds of rhubarb.

Then you chop the stalks into bite-sized chunks and dump all of that into a clean, preferably brand-new, plastic garbage pail big enough to hold all the rhubarb plus 16 quarts of lukewarm water.

Now stir in 8 to 10 pounds of sugar. Yes, I said 8 to 10 pounds of sugar. Here is where the experience of generations comes in. My grandma could tell if a particular year's rhubarb merited more or less sugar. The considered advice for first-timers or those with less-developed palates is to err on the side of less sugar.

Stir until the sugar is dissolved, then add the juice of 12 lemons. Yes, I know: this seems counterintuitive after trying to counteract rhubarb's tartness with all that sugar. But this is the recipe.

For color, Grandma recommended adding one or two packages of frozen raspberries.

Okay. Now cover the can and let this mixture sit for nine days, stirring once a day. After nine days, stir in more sugar—another 8 to 10 pounds. I said, another 8 to 10 pounds. You may get a sense of how your rhubarb is stacking up, tartness-wise, by now. (You may also get a sense of how important this ritual was, given that the price of sugar had to have varied over the years, often coming quite dear.)

Let this sit for nine more days, stirring once a day. After this, strain or siphon the resulting liquid into a large jug—the wine people call them *carboys,* available at a wine-making supply business, where you can also get an airlock, which improves the clarity of the wine.

Frankly, though, the women of Grandma's generation simply strained the liquid and poured it into jugs and bottles collected over the years and left the caps loosely screwed on, so the gases from the fermenting alcohol could escape. How many jugs and bottles, you ask? Well, you'll generally end up with about 20 quarts of wine. But the rhubarb may be especially juicy, or not. So it was never specified. Remember, these are the housewives who counseled, "Bake until done."

Then you wait. You can try drinking the wine in as little as three months, and you might be surprised. Likely, though, you're better off waiting until late November and then on through the winter. If you're really into this, you'll wait a year, always drinking the previous year's harvest.

Keep a log. Make some history. ◇

INDEX

almonds
In the Pink Shrimp Salad, 19–20
Spiced Couscous with Rhubarb
and Figs, 24
appetizers
Baked Camembert with Rhubarb
Compote, 18
Crostini with Goat Cheese, Prosciutto,
and Rhubarb Chutney, 17
Rhuba-dillas, 16
Shrimp in Kimonos, 14–15
apple
Baked Camembert with Rhubarb
Compote, 18
Salted Caramel Rhubapple Pie, 62–63
apricots
Crostini with Goat Cheese, Prosciutto,
and Rhubarb Chutney, 17
asparagus
Salmon and Rhubarb in Parchment
Packets, 42–43

bacon
Rhubarb-Bacon Compote, 28
Yorkshire Rhubarb, 27
Baked Camembert with Rhubarb Compote,
18
bananas
Rhubarb Foster, 79–80
basil
Rhubarb-Basil Cornmeal Cakes, 58–59
beer, dishes using, 41
Biscuits, Savory Rhubarb, 106–7
brandy, dishes using, 18, 96
breads and pastries. See also wonton/
potsticker wrappers
Cheese Biscuits, Rhubarb Cobbler with,
92–93

Crostini with Goat Cheese, Prosciutto,
and Rhubarb Chutney, 17
crusty bread, Baked Camembert
with Rhubarb Compote on, 18
Eastern Sky Scones, 102–3
Pork Morningside, 53–54
Rhubarb Crepe Cake, 70–71
Rhubarb Graham Muffins, 104
Rhubarb-Ricotta Turnovers, 84
Savory Rhubarb Biscuits, 106–7
Smoked Mozzarella Strudel with
Rhubarb Mostarda, 34–35
Zucchini-Rhubarb Bread, 108
Brine, 40
Browned Butter Rhubarb Sauce, 30
Burnt Creams, Rhubarb, 94–95

cakes
Gingery Rhubarb Upside-down Cake,
98–99
Persian Rhubarb Snack Cake, 88–89
Rhubarb-Basil Cornmeal Cakes, 58–59
Rhubarb Crepe Cake, 70–71
Rhubarb Pudding Cake, 56–57
Candied Walnuts, 18
caramel
Salted Caramel Rhubapple Pie, 62–63
champagne with Rhubarb Base, 111
cheese
Biscuits, Rhubarb Cobbler with, 92–93
Camembert, Baked, with Rhubarb
Compote, 18
Confetti Salad of Kale and Rhubarb, 23
Goat Cheese, Prosciutto, and Rhubarb
Chutney, Crostini with, 17
Rhuba-dillas (quesadillas), 16
Rhubarb-Ricotta Turnovers, 84
Savory Rhubarb Biscuits, 106–7

Smoked Mozzarella Strudel with
Rhubarb Mostarda, 34–35
Spiced Rhubarb-Squash Ravioli, 44–45
Spicy Chicken Breasts with Creamy
Rhubarb Sauce, 38–39
chicken and turkey
Chop-Chop Sweet and Sour Stir-fry,
48–49
Good Medicine Lettuce Wraps, 36–37
side dishes for, 24
Spicy Chicken Breasts with Creamy
Rhubarb Sauce, 38–39
Turkey Tenderloin with RhubarBQ
Sauce, 40–41
Chop-Chop Sweet and Sour Stir-fry, 48–49
Chutney, Rhubarb, Crostini with Goat
Cheese, Prosciutto, and, 17
Clafouti, Rhubarb-Raspberry, 96
Cobbler, Rhubarb, with Cheese Biscuits,
92–93
cocktails. *See* drinks
coconut
Coconut Crunch Torte with Rhubarb-
Pineapple Filling, 85–86
Rhubarb Graham Muffins, 104
Sawtooth Macaroons, 100
color variations in rhubarb, 56
Compote
Rhubarb
Baked Camembert with, 18
in Persian Rhubarb Snack Cake, 88–89
Rhubarb-Bacon, 28
condiments
Ketchup, Rhubarb, 29
Mostarda, 34
RhubarBQ Sauce, 41
Salsa, Mango-Rhubarb, 32–33
Confetti Salad of Kale and Rhubarb, 22–23
cookies
Rhubarb Meringue Tassies, 73–74
Sawtooth Macaroons, 100

corn
Fritters, Rhubarb, 25–26
Rhubarb-Basil Cornmeal Cakes, 58–59
Couscous, Spiced, with Rhubarb and Figs, 24
Crepe Cake, Rhubarb, 70–71
Crisps, Rhubarb, 68
Crostini with Goat Cheese, Prosciutto,
and Rhubarb Chutney, 17
crusts
Graham Cracker, 66
for Tassies, 73
Curd, Rhubarb, 69
as ingredient, 70–71, 73–74
Custard Pie, Rhubarb, 60

Dark 'n' Stormy (cocktail), 111
desserts
Coconut Crunch Torte with Rhubarb-
Pineapple Filling, 85–86
color variations in rhubarb and, 56
Frozen Roasted Rhubarb Meringue Pie,
66–67
Gingery Rhubarb Upside-down Cake,
98–99
Meringue, 74, 91
Orange Sponge Roulade with Rhubarb
Filling, 75–76
Persian Rhubarb Snack Cake, 88–89
Rhubarb-Basil Cornmeal Cakes, 58–59
Rhubarb Burnt Creams, 94–95
Rhubarb Cobbler with Cheese Biscuits,
92–93
Rhubarb Crepe Cake, 70–71
Rhubarb Crisp, 68
Rhubarb Curd, 69
as ingredient, 70–71, 73–74
Rhubarb Custard Pie, 60
Rhubarb Foster, 79–80
Rhubarb Meringue Tassies, 73–74
Rhubarb-Peach Pavlovas, 77–78
Rhubarb Pudding Cake, 56–57

desserts, *continued*
  Rhubarb-Raspberry Clafouti, 96
  Rhubarb-Ricotta Turnovers, 84
  Rhubarb Swirlygigs, 82–83
  Roasted Rhubarb-Ginger Granita, 87
  Salted Caramel Rhubapple Pie, 62–63
  Sawtooth Macaroons, 100
  Sour Cream–Rhubarb Torte with
    Meringue Topping, 90–91
  Strawberry-Rhubarb Pie, 64–65
  Streusel Topping, 62–63
drinks, alcoholic
  Rhubarb Wine, 112–13
  using Rhubarb Base, 110–11

Eastern Sky Scones, 102–3
entrees
  Chop-Chop Sweet and Sour Stir-fry,
    48–49
  Good Medicine Lettuce Wraps, 36–37
  Halibut Skewers with Mango-Rhubarb
    Salsa, 32–33
  Pork Loin Chops with Rhubarb Stuffing,
    47
  Pork Morningside, 53–54
  Rhubarb Khoresh, 51–52
  Salmon and Rhubarb in Parchment
    Packets, 42–43
  Smoked Mozzarella Strudel with
    Rhubarb Mostarda, 34–35
  Spiced Rhubarb-Squash Ravioli, 44–45
  Spicy Chicken Breasts with Creamy
    Rhubarb Sauce, 38–39
  Turkey Tenderloin with RhubarBQ
    Sauce, 40–41

figs
  Smoked Mozzarella Strudel with
    Rhubarb Mostarda, 34–35
  Spiced Couscous with Rhubarb
    and Figs, 24

fish
  Halibut Skewers with Mango-Rhubarb
    Salsa, 32–33
  Salmon and Rhubarb in Parchment
    Packets, 42–43
foundation recipes
  Savory Roasted Rhubarb, 8–9, 12
    as ingredient, 18, 53–54
  Sweet Roasted Rhubarb, 8, 11
    as ingredient, 66, 75–76, 77–78, 87
freezing of rhubarb, 8, 9
frozen rhubarb, commercial, 56
Frozen Roasted Rhubarb Meringue Pie,
    66–67
fruit
  apple
    Baked Camembert with Rhubarb
      Compote, 18
    Salted Caramel Rhubapple Pie, 62–63
  apricots
    Crostini with Goat Cheese, Prosciutto,
      and Rhubarb Chutney, 17
  figs
    Smoked Mozzarella Strudel with
      Rhubarb Mostarda, 34–35
    Spiced Couscous with Rhubarb
      and Figs, 24
  mango
    Eastern Sky Scones, 102–3
    Halibut Skewers with Mango-Rhubarb
      Salsa, 32–33
  peaches
    Rhubarb-Peach Pavlovas, 77–78
  pineapple
    Coconut Crunch Torte with Rhubarb-
      Pineapple Filling, 85–86
    Rhuba-dillas (quesadillas), 16
  raspberries
    Rhubarb-Raspberry Clafouti, 96
  strawberries
    Strawberry-Rhubarb Pie, 64–65

ginger
    Gingery Rhubarb Upside-down Cake, 98–99
    Roasted Rhubarb-Ginger Granita, 87
Glaze, Rhubarb, 59
Good Medicine Lettuce Wraps, 36–37
graham crackers
    Graham Cracker Crust, 66
    Rhubarb Graham Muffins, 104
grains
    Rhubarb Crisp, 68
    Spiced Couscous with Rhubarb and Figs, 24
Granita, Roasted Rhubarb-Ginger, 87
grilling
    fish
        Halibut Skewers with Mango-Rhubarb Salsa, 32–33
    meat
        condiments for, 29, 34
        side dishes for, 12, 24, 28
        Turkey Tenderloin with RhubarBQ Sauce, 40–41

Halibut Skewers with Mango-Rhubarb Salsa, 32–33

ice cream and granita
    desserts served with, 56–57, 68, 79–80, 82–83
    Roasted Rhubarb-Ginger Granita, 87
    toppings, 11
In the Pink Shrimp Salad, 19–20

jalapeño peppers
    Crostini with Goat Cheese, Prosciutto, and Rhubarb Chutney, 17
    Halibut Skewers with Mango-Rhubarb Salsa, 32–33
    Rhuba-dillas (quesadillas), 16

Kale and Rhubarb, Confetti Salad of, 22–23
Ketchup, Rhubarb, 29
    uses of, 41

lemons
    Quick Preserved Lemons, 52
lettuce
    Good Medicine Lettuce Wraps, 36–37
    In the Pink Shrimp Salad, 19–20

Macaroons, Sawtooth, 100
mango
    Eastern Sky Scones, 102–3
    Mango-Rhubarb Salsa, Halibut Skewers with, 32–33
meat
    bacon
        Rhubarb-Bacon Compote, 28
        Yorkshire Rhubarb, 27
    beef
        condiments for, 29
        side dishes for, 27
    chicken and turkey
        Chop-Chop Sweet and Sour Stir-fry, 48–49
        Good Medicine Lettuce Wraps, 36–37
        side dishes for, 24
        Spicy Chicken Breasts with Creamy Rhubarb Sauce, 38–39
        Turkey Tenderloin with RhubarBQ Sauce, 40–41
    grilled
        condiments for, 29, 34
        side dishes for, 12, 24, 28
        Turkey Tenderloin with RhubarBQ Sauce, 40–41
    lamb
        Rhubarb Khoresh, 51–52

meat, *continued*
    pork
        Loin Chops with Rhubarb Stuffing, 47
        Pork Morningside, 53–54
        side dishes for, 28
Meringue, 74, 91
    Rhubarb Meringue Tassies, 73–74
    Sour Cream–Rhubarb Torte with
        Meringue Topping, 90–91
Mostarda, Smoked Mozzarella Strudel
    with, 34–35
Muffins, Rhubarb Graham, 104

nuts
    almonds
        In the Pink Shrimp Salad, 19–20
        Spiced Couscous with Rhubarb
          and Figs, 24
    peanuts
        Good Medicine Lettuce Wraps, 36–37
    pistachios
        Persian Rhubarb Snack Cake, 88–89
    walnuts
        Candied Walnuts, 18
        Coconut Crunch Torte with Rhubarb-
          Pineapple Filling, 85–86
        Salted Caramel Rhubapple Pie, 62–63
    walnuts, candied
        Baked Camembert with Rhubarb
          Compote, 18
        Confetti Salad of Kale and Rhubarb,
          22–23

Orange Sponge Roulade with Rhubarb
    Filling, 75–76

parchment
    Salmon and Rhubarb in Parchment
        Packets, 42–43
pasta
    Spiced Rhubarb-Squash Ravioli, 44–45

Pavlovas, Rhubarb-Peach, 77–78
peaches
    Rhubarb-Peach Pavlovas, 77–78
Persian Rhubarb Snack Cake, 88–89
Pickled Rhubarb, 19, 22
pie
    Frozen Roasted Rhubarb Meringue Pie,
        66–67
    Rhubarb Custard Pie, 60
    Salted Caramel Rhubapple Pie, 62–63
    Strawberry-Rhubarb Pie, 64–65
pineapple
    Coconut Crunch Torte with Rhubarb-
        Pineapple Filling, 85–86
    Rhuba-dillas (quesadillas), 16
pomegranate molasses
    In the Pink Shrimp Salad, 19–20
    Persian Rhubarb Snack Cake, 88–89
    Turkey Tenderloin with RhubarBQ
        Sauce, 41
pork
    Pork Loin Chops with Rhubarb Stuffing,
        47
    Pork Morningside, 53–54
    side dishes for, 28
port, dishes using, 18
potsticker/wonton wrappers
    Shrimp in Kimonos, 14–15
    Spiced Rhubarb-Squash Ravioli, 44–45
poultry
    Chop-Chop Sweet and Sour Stir-fry,
        48–49
    Good Medicine Lettuce Wraps, 36–37
    side dishes for, 24
    Spicy Chicken Breasts with Creamy
        Rhubarb Sauce, 38–39
    Turkey Tenderloin with RhubarBQ
        Sauce, 40–41
Prosciutto, Crostini with Goat Cheese,
    Rhubarb Chutney and, 17

prosecco with Rhubarb Base, 111
Pudding Cake, Rhubarb, 56–57
puree
    of Savory Roasted Rhubarb, 12
    of Sweet Roasted Rhubarb, 11

quesadillas, rhubarb, pineapple
    and cheese, 16
Quick Preserved Lemons, 52

raspberries
    Rhubarb-Raspberry Clafouti, 96
Rhuba-dillas (quesadillas), 16
rhubarb
    botanical classification, 6
    history of use, 6
    misconceptions about, 5
    tartness of, 4–5, 6–8, 56
    versatility, 5
Rhubarb Base, 110–11
Rhubarb Bitters, 110
Rhubarb Curd, 69
    as ingredient, 70–71, 73–74
Rhubarb Filling, Orange Sponge Roulade
    with, 75–76
Rhubarb Foster, 79–80
Rhubarb-Pineapple Filling, Coconut
    Crunch Torte with, 85–86
RhubarBQ Sauce, Turkey Tenderloin with,
    40–41
Rhubarb Sauce, Creamy, Spicy Chicken
    Breasts with, 38–39
rice, Rhubarb Khoresh over, 51–52
Roasted Rhubarb
    Savory, 8–9, 12
        as ingredient, 18, 53–54
    Sweet, 8, 11
        as ingredient, 66, 75–76, 77–78, 87
Roasted Rhubarb-Ginger Granita, 87
Roulade, Orange Sponge, with Rhubarb
    Filling, 75–76

rum
    dishes using, 96
    with Rhubarb Base, 111

saffron
    Rhubarb Khoresh, 51–52
salads
    Confetti Salad of Kale and Rhubarb,
        22–23
    In the Pink Shrimp Salad, 19–20
Salmon and Rhubarb in Parchment
    Packets, 42–43
Salsa, Mango-Rhubarb, 32–33
Salted Caramel Rhubapple Pie, 62–63
sandwiches, condiments for, 29
sauces
    Browned Butter Rhubarb Sauce, 30
    Creamy Rhubarb Sauce, Spicy Chicken
        Breasts with, 38–39
    for Lettuce Wraps, 36
    Mango-Rhubarb Salsa, 32–33
    Rhubarb Curd, 69
    Rhubarb Glaze, 59
    RhubarBQ Sauce, Turkey Tenderloin
        with, 40–41
Savory Rhubarb Biscuits, 106–7
Savory Roasted Rhubarb, 8–9, 12
    as ingredient, 18, 53–54
Sawtooth Macaroons, 100
Scones, Eastern Sky, 102–3
shrimp
    Chop-Chop Sweet and Sour Stir-fry,
        48–49
    In the Pink Shrimp Salad, 19–20
    Shrimp in Kimonos, 14–15
side dishes
    Corn Fritters, Rhubarb, 25–26
    Rhubarb-Bacon Compote, 28
    Spiced Couscous with Rhubarb
        and Figs, 24
    Yorkshire Rhubarb, 27

Smoked Mozzarella Strudel with Rhubarb
    Mostarda, 34–35
Sour Cream–Rhubarb Torte with Meringue
    Topping, 90–91
Spiced Couscous with Rhubarb and Figs, 24
Spiced Rhubarb-Squash Ravioli, 44–45
Spicy Chicken Breasts with Creamy
    Rhubarb Sauce, 38–39
squash
    Spiced Rhubarb-Squash Ravioli, 44–45
    Zucchini-Rhubarb Bread, 108
stews
    Rhubarb Khoresh, 51–52
Strawberry-Rhubarb Pie, 64–65
Streusel Topping, 62–63
Strudel, Smoked Mozzarella, with Rhubarb
    Mostarda, 34–35
Stuffing, Rhubarb, Pork Loin Chops with, 47
Sweet Roasted Rhubarb, 8, 11
    as ingredient, 66, 75–76, 77–78, 87
Swirlygigs, Rhubarb, 82–83

torte
    Coconut Crunch, with Rhubarb-
        Pineapple Filling, 85–86
    Rhubarb Crepe Cake, 70–71
    Sour Cream–Rhubarb, with Meringue
        Topping, 90–91
Triple Sec
    Frozen Roasted Rhubarb Meringue Pie,
        66–67
turkey
    Good Medicine Lettuce Wraps, 36–37
    Turkey Tenderloin with RhubarBQ Sauce,
        40–41
Turnovers, Rhubarb-Ricotta, 84

vegetables, sauces for, 30
vodka
    with Rhubarb Base, 111
    Roasted Rhubarb-Ginger Granita, 87

walnuts
    Candied Walnuts, 18
    Coconut Crunch Torte with Rhubarb-
        Pineapple Filling, 85–86
    Salted Caramel Rhubapple Pie, 62–63
walnuts, candied
    Baked Camembert with Rhubarb
        Compote, 18
    Confetti Salad of Kale and Rhubarb,
        22–23
wine
    Halibut Skewers with Mango-Rhubarb
        Salsa, 32–33
    Rhubarb, 112–13
    Smoked Mozzarella Strudel with Rhubarb
        Mostarda, 34–35
    Spicy Chicken Breasts with Creamy
        Rhubarb Sauce, 38–39
wonton/potsticker wrappers
    Shrimp in Kimonos, 14–15
    Spiced Rhubarb-Squash Ravioli, 44–45

yogurt
    with Persian Rhubarb Snack Cake, 88–89
    Rhubarb Burnt Creams, 94–95
    with Rhubarb Khoresh, 51–52
Yorkshire Rhubarb, 27

Zucchini-Rhubarb Bread, 108